I Have, Who Has?

LANGUAGE ARTS

1–2

Written by

Trisha Callella

Editor: Jennifer Taylor

Cover Illustrator: Priscilla Burris

Production: Karen Nguyen

Art Director: Moonhee Pak

Project Director: Betsy Morris, PhD

Table of Contents

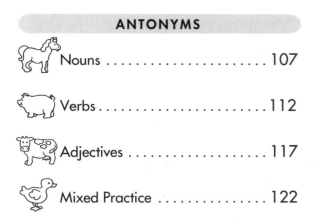
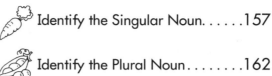

Introduction

I HAVE, WHO HAS? is a series of books that provides reinforcement for essential academic skills through group activities. These activities consist of game cards that students read and interactively answer. Each game also features an active listening enrichment activity. This component gives students additional practice in active listening and extends their learning to the application level.

I Have, Who Has? Language Arts 1–2 provides a fun, interactive way for students to practice various language arts skills. It includes 38 card games that will help improve students' auditory discrimination and reinforce standards-based language skills. The skills addressed in this resource include the following:

- Rhyming Words
- Word Families
- High Frequency Words
- Nouns
- Verbs
- Adjectives
- Vocabulary Development
- Synonyms

- Antonyms
- Analogies
- Contractions
- Compound Words
- Singular and Plural
- Main Idea
- Categorization
- Cause and Effect

The ease and simplicity of preparing these games for your class will allow you to begin using *I Have, Who Has?* today! These engaging games are sure to keep students involved as they are learning valuable language arts skills.

ORGANIZATION

Each card game consists of 32 question and answer cards. The cards are arranged in columns (top to bottom) in the order they will be read by the class. A reproducible active listening enrichment page follows every set of game cards. Play the interactive card games alone or in conjunction with this reproducible page to reinforce children's active listening, increase active participation, provide enrichment, and extend the learning and accountability of each child.

INSTRUCTIONS FOR I HAVE, WHO HAS GAME CARDS

1) Photocopy two sets of the game cards. Keep one copy as your reference to the correct order of questions and answers.

2) Cut apart the second set of game cards. Mix up the cards and pass them out to the children. Every child should have at least one card. Depending on your class size, children may have more than one card.

3) Have the student with the first card begin the game by saying *I have the first card. Who has...?* As each student reads a card, monitor your copy to make sure children are reading the cards in the correct order. If children correctly matched each card, then the last card read will "loop" back to the first card and read *I have... Who has the first card?*

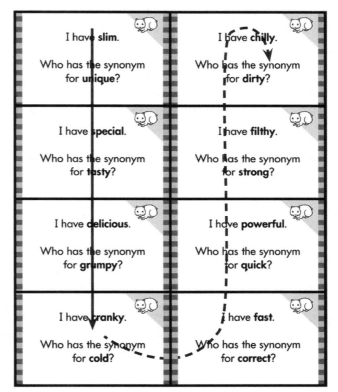

INSTRUCTIONS FOR ACTIVE LISTENING ENRICHMENT PAGE

1) Copy one page for each child or pair of children.

2) Make sure each child has a light-colored crayon or highlighter (not a marker or pencil) to color over the correct boxes as they are read. Provide time for children to lightly color or highlight the correct box.

3) Some of the activity pages contain a riddle. After the last card is read, ask children to uncover the hidden text (e.g., riddle, proverb) by reading the text in all of the boxes they did not color or highlight. Have them read from top to bottom and from left to right on the grid. Then, have them answer the extension questions at the bottom of the page. Use the answer key on pages 197-203 to check children's answers.

WHAT TO OBSERVE

1) Children who have difficulty locating the correct boxes on the active listening enrichment page once familiarity with the format has been established may have difficulties with visual discrimination.

2) Children who have difficulty reading their cards at the correct time may have difficulties with attention, hearing, active listening, or the concepts being reinforced.

VARIATIONS
(To be played without the active listening enrichment page)

Timed Version

Have children play the game twice. Encourage them to beat their time in the second round. Have children play the same game again the next day. Can they beat their time again? Remember to mix up the cards before distributing them for each new game.

Small Groups

Give each group a set of game cards. Encourage groups to pay close attention, read quickly, and stay on task to determine which group is the fastest. Playing in smaller groups allows children to have more cards. This raises the opportunities for individual accountability, active participation, time on task, and reinforcement per child.

Card Reduction

If your class is not ready to play with multiple cards, you can reduce the number to fit your class needs. Photocopy the set of the game cards you want to play. Determine the appropriate number of cards needed. Following the existing order of the game, begin with the first card and count the number of cards you need. Delete the *Who has...?* clue from the last card counted and replace with the sentence *Who has the first card?* Photocopy and cut apart the revised game for class play.

One-Syllable Rhyming Words

I have the **first card**.

Who has the word that rhymes with **hat**?

I have **stop**.

Who has the word that rhymes with **see**?

I have **bat**.

Who has the word that rhymes with **bunk**?

I have **free**.

Who has the word that rhymes with **red**?

I have **trunk**.

Who has the word that rhymes with **sun**?

I have **bed**.

Who has the word that rhymes with **big**?

I have **fun**.

Who has the word that rhymes with **hop**?

I have **pig**.

Who has the word that rhymes with **day**?

One-Syllable Rhyming Words

I have **play**.

Who has the word that rhymes with **hot**?

I have **hug**.

Who has the word that rhymes with **pin**?

I have **not**.

Who has the word that rhymes with **back**?

I have **chin**.

Who has the word that rhymes with **man**?

I have **sack**.

Who has the word that rhymes with **ring**?

I have **ran**.

Who has the word that rhymes with **best**?

I have **sing**.

Who has the word that rhymes with **bug**?

I have **rest**.

Who has the word that rhymes with **rock**?

I Have, Who Has?: Language Arts • 1–2 © 2007 Creative Teaching Press

One-Syllable Rhyming Words

I have **sock**.

Who has the word that rhymes with **make**?

I have **glad**.

Who has the word that rhymes with **mail**?

I have **take**.

Who has the word that rhymes with **duck**?

I have **tail**.

Who has the word that rhymes with **call**?

I have **luck**.

Who has the word that rhymes with **face**?

I have **fall**.

Who has the word that rhymes with **tap**?

I have **race**.

Who has the word that rhymes with **dad**?

I have **map**.

Who has the word that rhymes with **dark**?

One-Syllable Rhyming Words

I have **park**.

Who has the word that rhymes with **part**?

I have **seal**.

Who has the word that rhymes with **feed**?

I have **smart**.

Who has the word that rhymes with **heat**?

I have **seed**.

Who has the word that rhymes with **time**?

I have **treat**.

Who has the word that rhymes with **save**?

I have **dime**.

Who has the word that rhymes with **send**?

I have **gave**.

Who has the word that rhymes with **meal**?

I have **bend**.

Who has the **first card**?

I Have, Who Has?: Language Arts • 1–2 © 2007 Creative Teaching Press

Name _____ Date _____

One-Syllable Rhyming Words

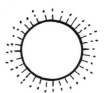

I Follow the path by coloring the words as your classmates name them.

*Start	bat	stop	free	bed
ball	trunk	fun	play	pig
fall	tail	glad	not	sack
map	snake	race	she	sing
park	smart	luck	take	hug
gave	treat	sled	sock	chin
seal	log	*Finish	rest	ran
seed	dime	bend	hug	cat

II Write four words that are not colored in the table. Write a rhyme for each.

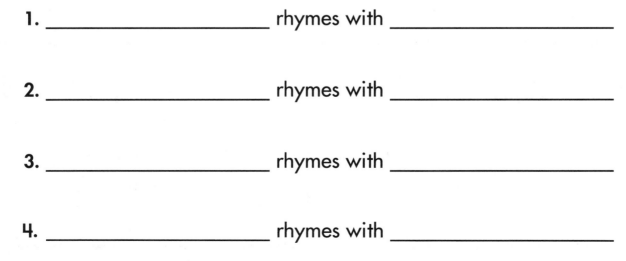

1. _____ rhymes with _____

2. _____ rhymes with _____

3. _____ rhymes with _____

4. _____ rhymes with _____

Two-Syllable Rhyming Words

I have the **first card**.

Who has the word that rhymes with **table**?

I have **power**.

Who has the word that rhymes with **kitten**?

I have **cable**.

Who has the word that rhymes with **treasure**?

I have **mitten**.

Who has the word that rhymes with **shoulder**?

I have **measure**.

Who has the word that rhymes with **puddle**?

I have **boulder**.

Who has the word that rhymes with **spider**?

I have **huddle**.

Who has the word that rhymes with **tower**?

I have **glider**.

Who has the word that rhymes with **honey**?

I Have, Who Has?: Language Arts • 1–2 © 2007 Creative Teaching Press

Two-Syllable Rhyming Words

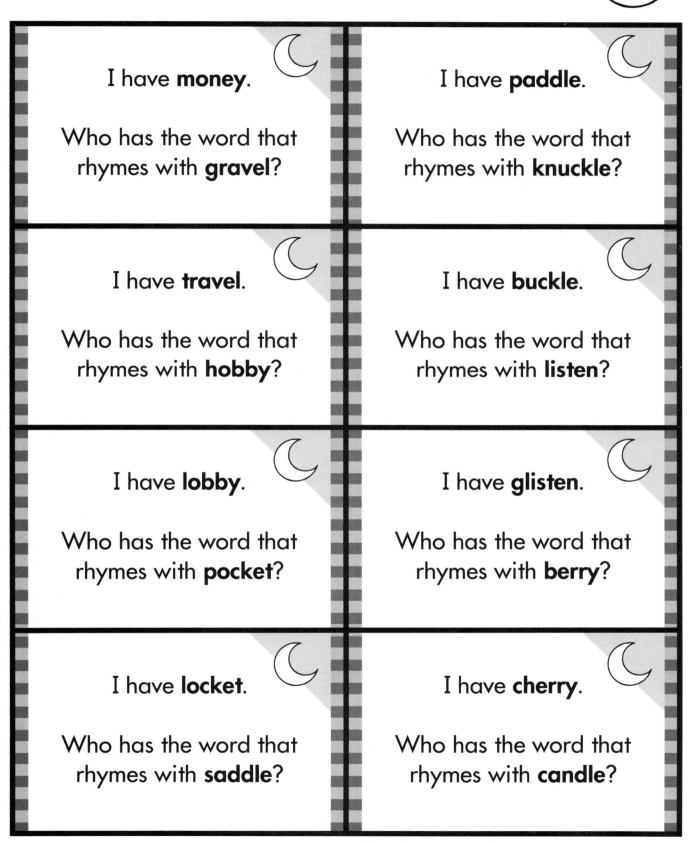

I have **money**.

Who has the word that rhymes with **gravel**?

I have **paddle**.

Who has the word that rhymes with **knuckle**?

I have **travel**.

Who has the word that rhymes with **hobby**?

I have **buckle**.

Who has the word that rhymes with **listen**?

I have **lobby**.

Who has the word that rhymes with **pocket**?

I have **glisten**.

Who has the word that rhymes with **berry**?

I have **locket**.

Who has the word that rhymes with **saddle**?

I have **cherry**.

Who has the word that rhymes with **candle**?

Two-Syllable Rhyming Words

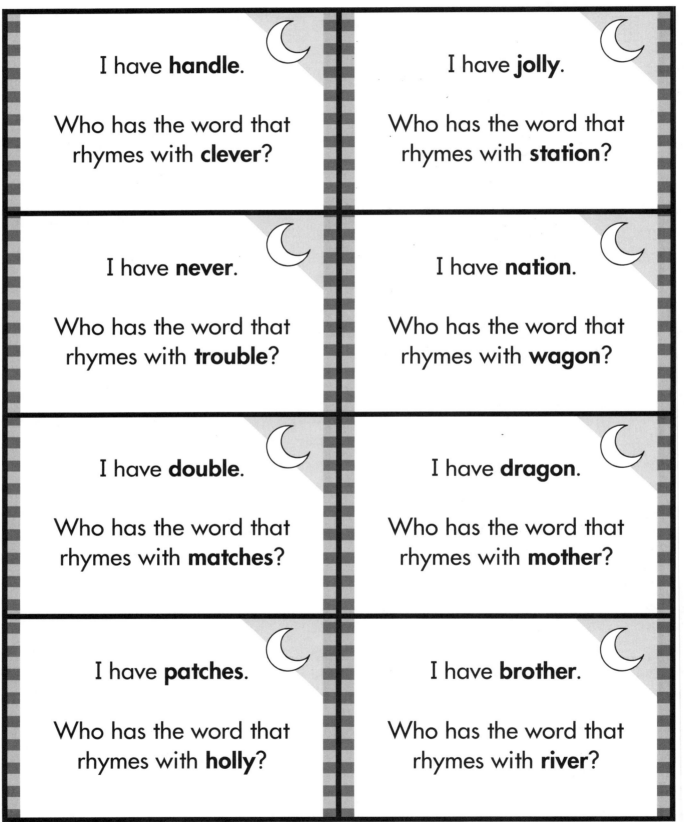

I have **handle**.

Who has the word that rhymes with **clever**?

I have **jolly**.

Who has the word that rhymes with **station**?

I have **never**.

Who has the word that rhymes with **trouble**?

I have **nation**.

Who has the word that rhymes with **wagon**?

I have **double**.

Who has the word that rhymes with **matches**?

I have **dragon**.

Who has the word that rhymes with **mother**?

I have **patches**.

Who has the word that rhymes with **holly**?

I have **brother**.

Who has the word that rhymes with **river**?

I Have, Who Has?: Language Arts • 1–2 © 2007 Creative Teaching Press

Two-Syllable Rhyming Words

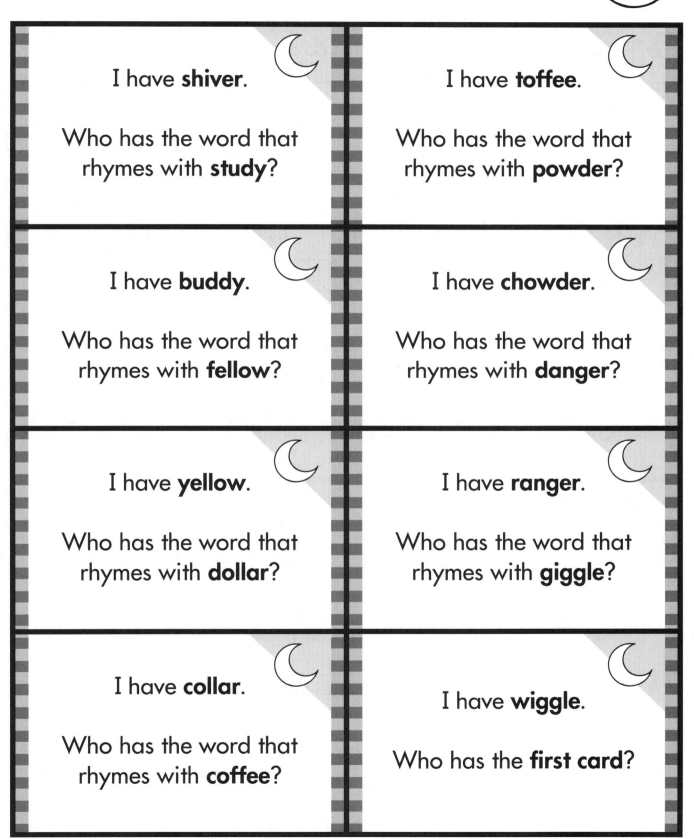

I have **shiver**.

Who has the word that rhymes with **study**?

I have **toffee**.

Who has the word that rhymes with **powder**?

I have **buddy**.

Who has the word that rhymes with **fellow**?

I have **chowder**.

Who has the word that rhymes with **danger**?

I have **yellow**.

Who has the word that rhymes with **dollar**?

I have **ranger**.

Who has the word that rhymes with **giggle**?

I have **collar**.

Who has the word that rhymes with **coffee**?

I have **wiggle**.

Who has the **first card**?

Two-Syllable Rhyming Words

I Follow the path by coloring the words as your classmates name them.

*Start	cable	measure	guppy
buckle	paddle	huddle	power
glisten	locket	flurry	mitten
cherry	lobby	travel	boulder
handle	never	money	glider
honey	double	patches	jolly
yellow	buddy	hazy	nation
collar	shiver	brother	dragon
toffee	blubber	*Finish	manner
chowder	ranger	wiggle	flower

II Write four words that are not colored in the table. Write a rhyme for each.

1. _____ rhymes with _____

2. _____ rhymes with _____

3. _____ rhymes with _____

4. _____ rhymes with _____

Basic Word Families

I have the **first card**.

Who has three words that are in the same word family as **day**?

I have **luck**, **buck**, and **stuck**.

Who has three words that are in the same word family as **him**?

I have **say**, **play**, and **way**.

Who has three words that are in the same word family as **gum**?

I have **rim**, **brim**, and **grim**.

Who has three words that are in the same word family as **dip**?

I have **hum**, **drum**, and **plum**.

Who has three words that are in the same word family as **hill**?

I have **ship**, **hip**, and **slip**.

Who has three words that are in the same word family as **cat**?

I have **will**, **fill**, and **pill**.

Who has three words that are in the same word family as **duck**?

I have **rat**, **sat**, and **flat**.

Who has three words that are in the same word family as **ram**?

I Have, Who Has?: Language Arts • 1–2 © 2007 Creative Teaching Press

Basic Word Families

I have **ham**, **clam**, and **jam**.

Who has three words that are in the same word family as **bag**?

I have **sank**, **tank**, and **blank**.

Who has three words that are in the same word family as **bell**?

I have **tag**, **rag**, and **wag**.

Who has three words that are in the same word family as **back**?

I have **fell**, **sell**, and **well**.

Who has three words that are in the same word family as **pot**?

I have **sack**, **black**, and **rack**.

Who has three words that are in the same word family as **pick**?

I have **not**, **got**, and **hot**.

Who has three words that are in the same word family as **ring**?

I have **sick**, **click**, and **quick**.

Who has three words that are in the same word family as **bank**?

I have **sing**, **thing**, and **bring**.

Who has three words that are in the same word family as **cap**?

Basic Word Families

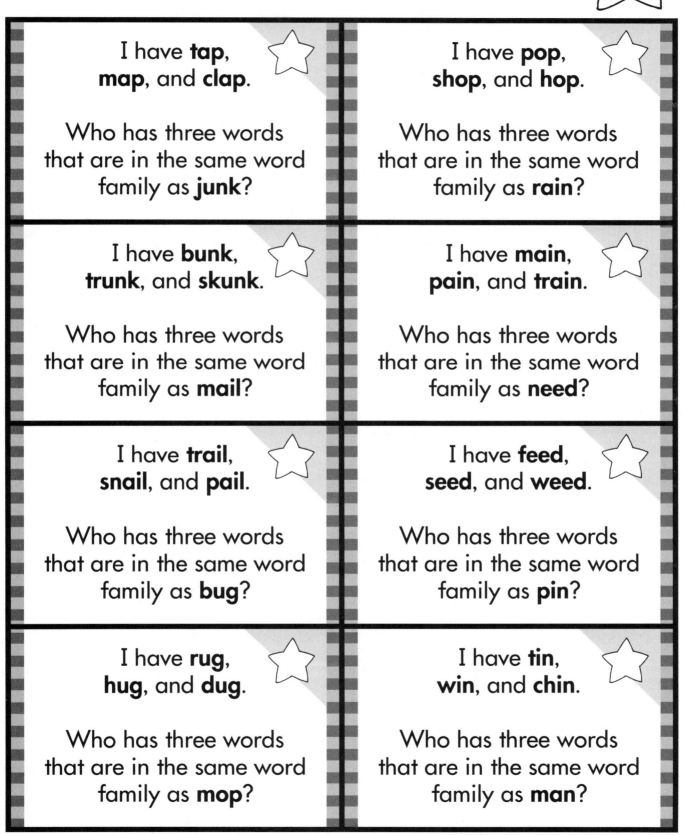

I have **tap**, **map**, and **clap**.

Who has three words that are in the same word family as **junk**?

I have **pop**, **shop**, and **hop**.

Who has three words that are in the same word family as **rain**?

I have **bunk**, **trunk**, and **skunk**.

Who has three words that are in the same word family as **mail**?

I have **main**, **pain**, and **train**.

Who has three words that are in the same word family as **need**?

I have **trail**, **snail**, and **pail**.

Who has three words that are in the same word family as **bug**?

I have **feed**, **seed**, and **weed**.

Who has three words that are in the same word family as **pin**?

I have **rug**, **hug**, and **dug**.

Who has three words that are in the same word family as **mop**?

I have **tin**, **win**, and **chin**.

Who has three words that are in the same word family as **man**?

Basic Word Families

I have **pan**, **ran**, and **tan**.

Who has three words that are in the same word family as **best**?

I have **grow**, **slow**, and **snow**.

Who has three words that are in the same word family as **new**?

I have **nest**, **rest**, and **test**.

Who has three words that are in the same word family as **pink**?

I have **few**, **chew**, and **grew**.

Who has three words that are in the same word family as **more**?

I have **sink**, **drink**, and **think**.

Who has three words that are in the same word family as **my**?

I have **sore**, **tore**, and **chore**.

Who has three words that are in the same word family as **red**?

I have **by**, **try**, and **fly**.

Who has three words that are in the same word family as **show**?

I have **bed**, **fed**, and **led**.

Who has the **first card**?

I Have, Who Has?: Language Arts • 1–2 © 2007 Creative Teaching Press

Name _____ Date _____

Basic Word Families

I Follow the path by coloring the words as your classmates name them.

*Start	rug hug dug	trail snail pail	bunk trunk skunk	tap map clap	sing thing bring
say play way	pop shop hop	main pain train	feed seed weed	tin win chin	not got hot
hum drum plum				pan ran tan	fell sell well
will fill pill	sore tore chore	bed fed led	*Finish	nest rest test	sank tank blank
luck buck stuck	few chew grew	grow slow snow	by try fly	sink drink think	sick click quick
rim brim grim	ship hip slip	rat sat flat	ham clam jam	tag rag wag	sack black rack

II Within each box circle the part of the word that is the same.

III Choose a word family. Write three more words for that family in the empty space.

Short Vowel Word Families

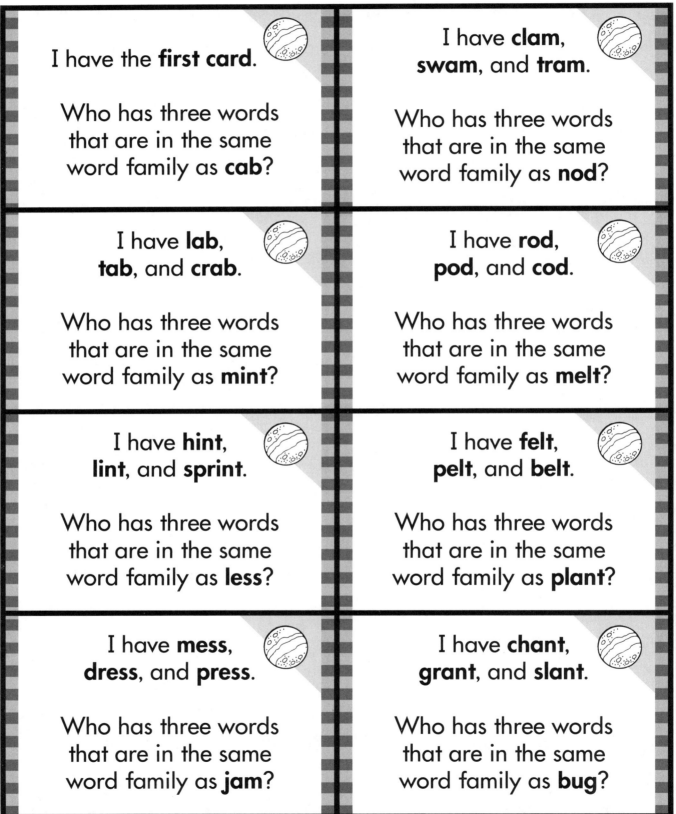

I have the **first card**.

Who has three words that are in the same word family as **cab**?

I have **clam**, **swam**, and **tram**.

Who has three words that are in the same word family as **nod**?

I have **lab**, **tab**, and **crab**.

Who has three words that are in the same word family as **mint**?

I have **rod**, **pod**, and **cod**.

Who has three words that are in the same word family as **melt**?

I have **hint**, **lint**, and **sprint**.

Who has three words that are in the same word family as **less**?

I have **felt**, **pelt**, and **belt**.

Who has three words that are in the same word family as **plant**?

I have **mess**, **dress**, and **press**.

Who has three words that are in the same word family as **jam**?

I have **chant**, **grant**, and **slant**.

Who has three words that are in the same word family as **bug**?

I Have, Who Has?: Language Arts • 1–2 © 2007 Creative Teaching Press

Short Vowel Word Families

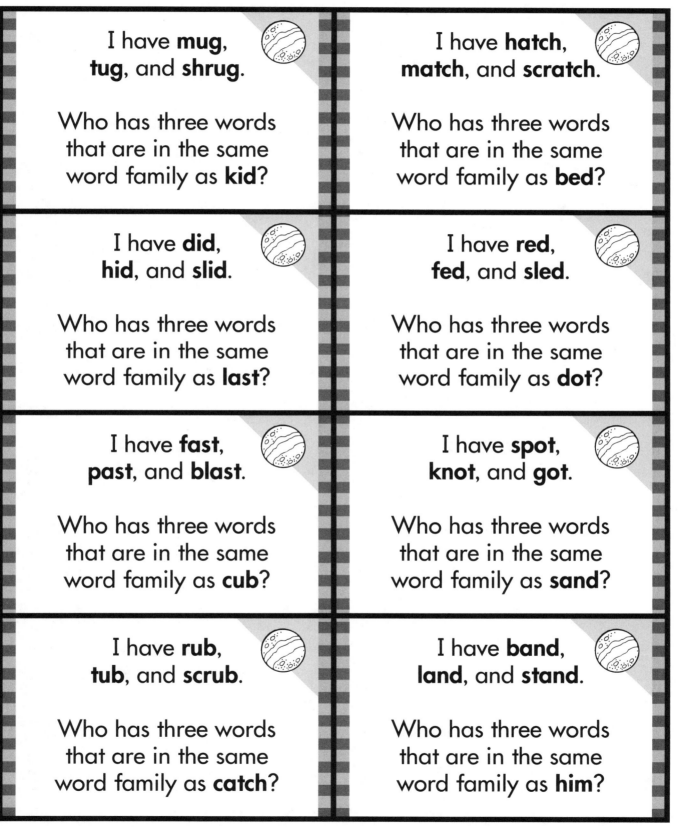

I have **mug**, **tug**, and **shrug**.

Who has three words that are in the same word family as **kid**?

I have **hatch**, **match**, and **scratch**.

Who has three words that are in the same word family as **bed**?

I have **did**, **hid**, and **slid**.

Who has three words that are in the same word family as **last**?

I have **red**, **fed**, and **sled**.

Who has three words that are in the same word family as **dot**?

I have **fast**, **past**, and **blast**.

Who has three words that are in the same word family as **cub**?

I have **spot**, **knot**, and **got**.

Who has three words that are in the same word family as **sand**?

I have **rub**, **tub**, and **scrub**.

Who has three words that are in the same word family as **catch**?

I have **band**, **land**, and **stand**.

Who has three words that are in the same word family as **him**?

Short Vowel Word Families

I have **rim**, **swim**, and **trim**.

Who has three words that are in the same word family as **send**?

I have **test**, **west**, and **chest**.

Who has three words that are in the same word family as **get**?

I have **bend**, **spend**, and **trend**.

Who has three words that are in the same word family as **luck**?

I have **pet**, **met**, and **wet**.

Who has three words that are in the same word family as **sick**?

I have **truck**, **stuck**, and **duck**.

Who has three words that are in the same word family as **dad**?

I have **pick**, **trick**, and **chick**.

Who has three words that are in the same word family as **rash**?

I have **sad**, **had**, and **lad**.

Who has three words that are in the same word family as **pest**?

I have **trash**, **smash**, and **flash**.

Who has three words that are in the same word family as **big**?

I Have, Who Has?: Language Arts • 1–2 © 2007 Creative Teaching Press

Short Vowel Word Families

I have **pig**, **dig**, and **twig**.

Who has three words that are in the same word family as **men**?

I have **dock**, **flock**, and **shock**.

Who has three words that are in the same word family as **list**?

I have **hen**, **ten**, and **when**.

Who has three words that are in the same word family as **win**?

I have **fist**, **twist**, and **wrist**.

Who has three words that are in the same word family as **job**?

I have **pin**, **skin**, and **twin**.

Who has three words that are in the same word family as **back**?

I have **slob**, **mob**, and **knob**.

Who has three words that are in the same word family as **dip**?

I have **lack**, **sack**, and **black**.

Who has three words that are in the same word family as **clock**?

I have **lip**, **chip**, and **flip**.

Who has the **first card**?

I Have, Who Has?: Language Arts • 1–2 © 2007 Creative Teaching Press

Name _____ Date _____

Short Vowel Word Families

I Follow the path by coloring the words as your classmates name them.

*Start				*Finish	lip chip flip
lab tab crab	pin skin twin	lack sack black	dock flock shock	fist twist wrist	slob mob knob
hint lint sprint	hen ten when	pick trick chick	pet met wet	truck stuck duck	bend spend trend
mess dress press	pig dig twig	trash smash flash	test west chest	sad had lad	rim swim trim
clam swam tram	chant grant slant	mug tug shrug	rub tub scrub	hatch match scratch	band land stand
rod pod cod	felt pelt belt	did hid slid	fast past blast	red fed sled	spot knot got

II Within each box circle the part of the word that is the same.

III Choose a word family. Write three more words for that family in the empty space.

I Have, Who Has?: Language Arts • 1–2 © 2007 Creative Teaching Press

Long Vowel Word Families

I have the **first card**.

Who has three words that are in the same word family as **race**?

I have **mail**, **snail**, and **quail**.

Who has three words that are in the same word family as **hide**?

I have **face**, **place**, and **trace**.

Who has three words that are in the same word family as **neat**?

I have **side**, **ride**, and **pride**.

Who has three words that are in the same word family as **deal**?

I have **treat**, **heat**, and **wheat**.

Who has three words that are in the same word family as **boat**?

I have **heal**, **seal**, and **meal**.

Who has three words that are in the same word family as **find**?

I have **goat**, **float**, and **throat**.

Who has three words that are in the same word family as **tail**?

I have **kind**, **grind**, and **blind**.

Who has three words that are in the same word family as **flown**?

I Have, Who Has? Language Arts • 1–2 © 2007 Creative Teaching Press

Long Vowel Word Families

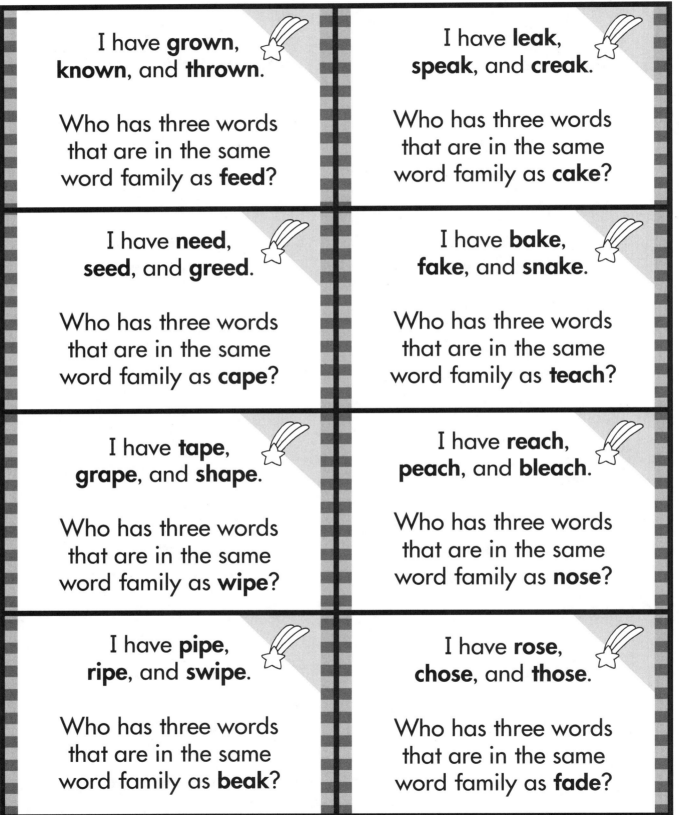

I have **grown**, **known**, and **thrown**.

Who has three words that are in the same word family as **feed**?

I have **leak**, **speak**, and **creak**.

Who has three words that are in the same word family as **cake**?

I have **need**, **seed**, and **greed**.

Who has three words that are in the same word family as **cape**?

I have **bake**, **fake**, and **snake**.

Who has three words that are in the same word family as **teach**?

I have **tape**, **grape**, and **shape**.

Who has three words that are in the same word family as **wipe**?

I have **reach**, **peach**, and **bleach**.

Who has three words that are in the same word family as **nose**?

I have **pipe**, **ripe**, and **swipe**.

Who has three words that are in the same word family as **beak**?

I have **rose**, **chose**, and **those**.

Who has three words that are in the same word family as **fade**?

I Have, Who Has?: Language Arts • 1–2 © 2007 Creative Teaching Press

Long Vowel Word Families

I have **jade**, **shade**, and **trade**.

Who has three words that are in the same word family as **tree**?

I have **mice**, **twice**, and **slice**.

Who has three words that are in the same word family as **train**?

I have **free**, **bee**, and **knee**.

Who has three words that are in the same word family as **blow**?

I have **chain**, **drain**, and **brain**.

Who has three words that are in the same word family as **life**?

I have **flow**, **snow**, and **grow**.

Who has three words that are in the same word family as **deep**?

I have **wife**, **strife**, and **knife**.

Who has three words that are in the same word family as **rope**?

I have **keep**, **sheep**, and **sleep**.

Who has three words that are in the same word family as **rice**?

I have **hope**, **scope**, and **slope**.

Who has three words that are in the same word family as **bike**?

Long Vowel Word Families

I have **hike, like,** and **strike**.

Who has three words that are in the same word family as **joke**?

I have **hire, tire,** and **wire**.

Who has three words that are in the same word family as **hive**?

I have **broke, choke,** and **spoke**.

Who has three words that are in the same word family as **dime**?

I have **dive, five,** and **drive**.

Who has three words that are in the same word family as **toast**?

I have **lime, time,** and **slime**.

Who has three words that are in the same word family as **came**?

I have **roast, boast,** and **coast**.

Who has three words that are in the same word family as **page**?

I have **name, same,** and **game**.

Who has three words that are in the same word family as **fire**?

I have **wage, cage,** and **stage**.

Who has the **first card**?

I Have, Who Has?: Language Arts • 1–2 © 2007 Creative Teaching Press

Name _____ Date _____

Long Vowel Word Families

I Follow the path by coloring the words as your classmates name them.

*Start	face place trace	treat heat wheat	goat float throat	flow snow grow	keep sheep sleep
kind grind blind	heal seal meal	side ride pride	mail snail quail	free bee knee	mice twice slice
grown known thrown	pipe ripe swipe	leak speak creak	rose chose those	jade shade trade	chain drain brain
need seed greed	tape grape shape	bake fake snake	reach peach bleach	hope scope slope	wife strife knife
*Finish	wage cage stage	roast boast coast	dive five drive	hike like strike	broke choke spoke
			hire tire wire	name same game	lime time slime

II Within each box circle the part of the word that is the same.

III Choose a word family. Write three more words for that family in the empty space.

I Have, Who Has?: Language Arts • 1–2 © 2007 Creative Teaching Press

Advanced Word Families

I have the **first card**.

Who has three words that are in the same word family as **raft**?

I have **roast**, **boast**, and **toast**.

Who has three words that are in the same word family as **limp**?

I have **craft**, **draft**, and **shaft**.

Who has three words that are in the same word family as **moth**?

I have **chimp**, **blimp**, and **skimp**.

Who has three words that are in the same word family as **walk**?

I have **broth**, **cloth**, and **sloth**.

Who has three words that are in the same word family as **faint**?

I have **talk**, **chalk**, and **stalk**.

Who has three words that are in the same word family as **wedge**?

I have **paint**, **saint**, and **quaint**.

Who has three words that are in the same word family as **coast**?

I have **hedge**, **pledge**, and **ledge**.

Who has three words that are in the same word family as **dance**?

I Have, Who Has?: Language Arts • 1–2 © 2007 Creative Teaching Press

Advanced Word Families

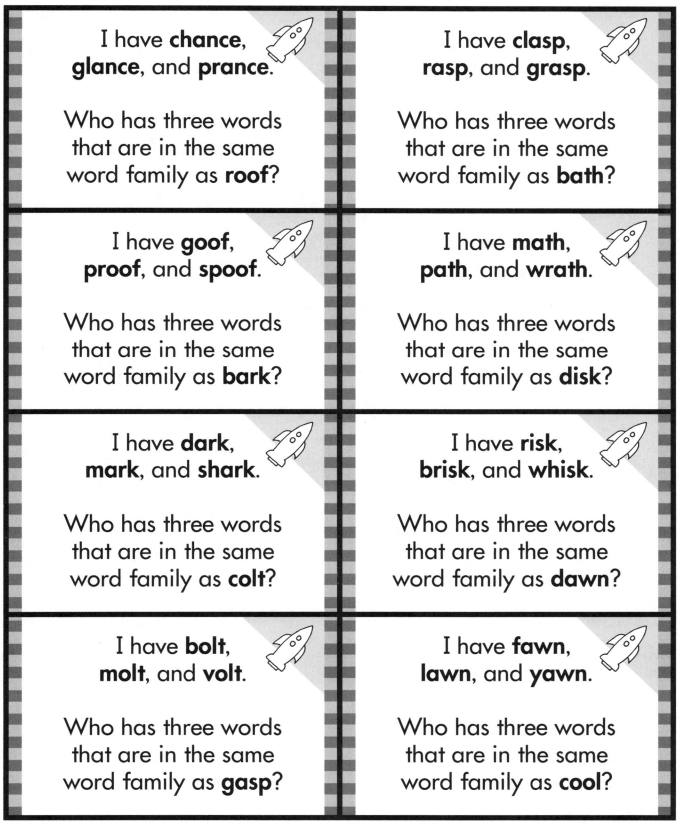

I have **chance**, **glance**, and **prance**.

Who has three words that are in the same word family as **roof**?

I have **clasp**, **rasp**, and **grasp**.

Who has three words that are in the same word family as **bath**?

I have **goof**, **proof**, and **spoof**.

Who has three words that are in the same word family as **bark**?

I have **math**, **path**, and **wrath**.

Who has three words that are in the same word family as **disk**?

I have **dark**, **mark**, and **shark**.

Who has three words that are in the same word family as **colt**?

I have **risk**, **brisk**, and **whisk**.

Who has three words that are in the same word family as **dawn**?

I have **bolt**, **molt**, and **volt**.

Who has three words that are in the same word family as **gasp**?

I have **fawn**, **lawn**, and **yawn**.

Who has three words that are in the same word family as **cool**?

I Have, Who Has? Language Arts • 1–2 © 2007 Creative Teaching Press

Advanced Word Families

I have **pool**, **tool**, and **school**.

Who has three words that are in the same word family as **reach**?

I have **cream**, **stream**, and **team**.

Who has three words that are in the same word family as **damp**?

I have **teach**, **beach**, and **peach**.

Who has three words that are in the same word family as **bought**?

I have **camp**, **champ**, and **stamp**.

Who has three words that are in the same word family as **bench**?

I have **fought**, **brought**, and **thought**.

Who has three words that are in the same word family as **task**?

I have **trench**, **wrench**, and **French**.

Who has three words that are in the same word family as **wait**?

I have **mask**, **bask**, and **cask**.

Who has three words that are in the same word family as **dream**?

I have **trait**, **gait**, and **bait**.

Who has three words that are in the same word family as **since**?

I Have, Who Has?: Language Arts • 1–2 © 2007 Creative Teaching Press

Advanced Word Families

I have **mince**, **wince**, and **prince**.

Who has three words that are in the same word family as **saw**?

I have **coil**, **foil**, and **soil**.

Who has three words that are in the same word family as **part**?

I have **jaw**, **flaw**, and **gnaw**.

Who has three words that are in the same word family as **roach**?

I have **cart**, **smart**, and **start**.

Who has three words that are in the same word family as **long**?

I have **coach**, **poach**, and **broach**.

Who has three words that are in the same word family as **chair**?

I have **wrong**, **strong**, and **prong**.

Who has three words that are in the same word family as **good**?

I have **stair**, **fair**, and **hair**.

Who has three words that are in the same word family as **boil**?

I have **wood**, **hood**, and **stood**.

Who has the **first card**?

I Have, Who Has?: Language Arts • 1–2 © 2007 Creative Teaching Press

Advanced Word Families

I Follow the path by coloring the words as your classmates name them.

*Start	craft draft shaft	broth cloth sloth	paint saint quaint	roast boast toast	chimp blimp skimp
fawn lawn yawn	risk brisk whisk	math path wrath	clasp rasp grasp	bolt molt volt	talk chalk stalk
pool tool school	mask bask cask	cream stream team	camp champ stamp	dark mark shark	hedge pledge ledge
teach beach peach	fought brought thought	trait gait bait	trench wrench French	goof proof spoof	chance glance prance
coach poach broach	jaw flaw gnaw	mince wince prince			
stair fair hair	coil foil soil	cart smart start	wrong strong prong	wood hood stood	*Finish

II Within each box circle the part of the word that is the same.

III Choose a word family. Write three more words for that family in the empty space.

I Have, Who Has?: Language Arts • 1–2 © 2007 Creative Teaching Press

Spelling 1

I have the **first card**.

Who has the spelling for the word **the**?

I have **i – n**.

Who has the spelling for the word **is**?

I have **t – h – e**.

Who has the spelling for the word **and**?

I have **i – s**.

Who has the spelling for the word **he**?

I have **a – n – d**.

Who has the spelling for the word **to**?

I have **h – e**.

Who has the spelling for the word **for**?

I have **t – o**.

Who has the spelling for the word **in**?

I have **f – o – r**.

Who has the spelling for the word **you**?

Spelling 1

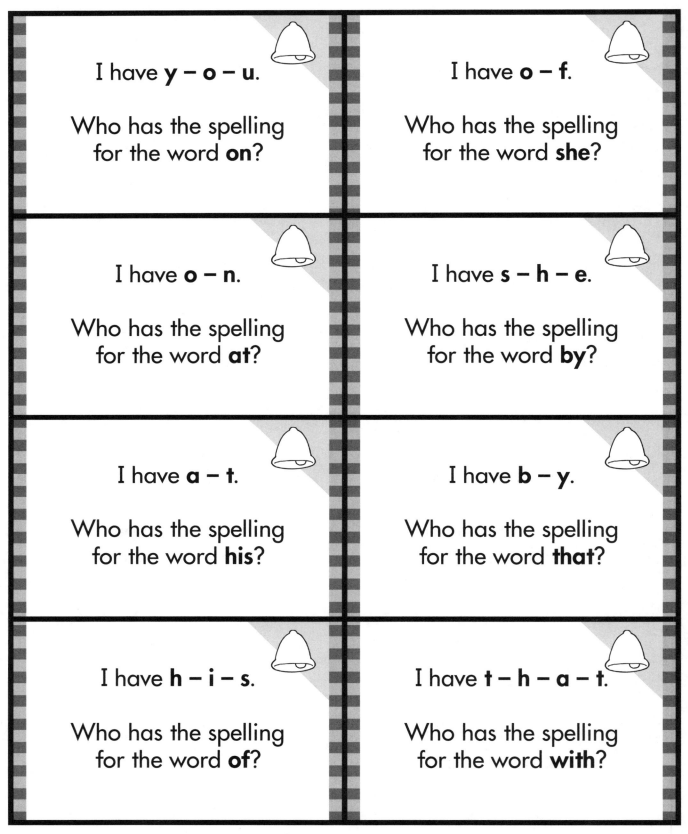

I have **y – o – u**.

Who has the spelling for the word **on**?

I have **o – f**.

Who has the spelling for the word **she**?

I have **o – n**.

Who has the spelling for the word **at**?

I have **s – h – e**.

Who has the spelling for the word **by**?

I have **a – t**.

Who has the spelling for the word **his**?

I have **b – y**.

Who has the spelling for the word **that**?

I have **h – i – s**.

Who has the spelling for the word **of**?

I have **t – h – a – t**.

Who has the spelling for the word **with**?

I Have, Who Has?: Language Arts • 1–2 © 2007 Creative Teaching Press

Spelling 1

I have **w – i – t – h**.

Who has the spelling for the word **have**?

I have **t – h – e – y**.

Who has the spelling for the word **had**?

I have **h – a – v – e**.

Who has the spelling for the word **from**?

I have **h – a – d**.

Who has the spelling for the word **do**?

I have **f – r – o – m**.

Who has the spelling for the word **this**?

I have **d – o**.

Who has the spelling for the word **but**?

I have **t – h – i – s**.

Who has the spelling for the word **they**?

I have **b – u – t**.

Who has the spelling for the word **not**?

Spelling 1

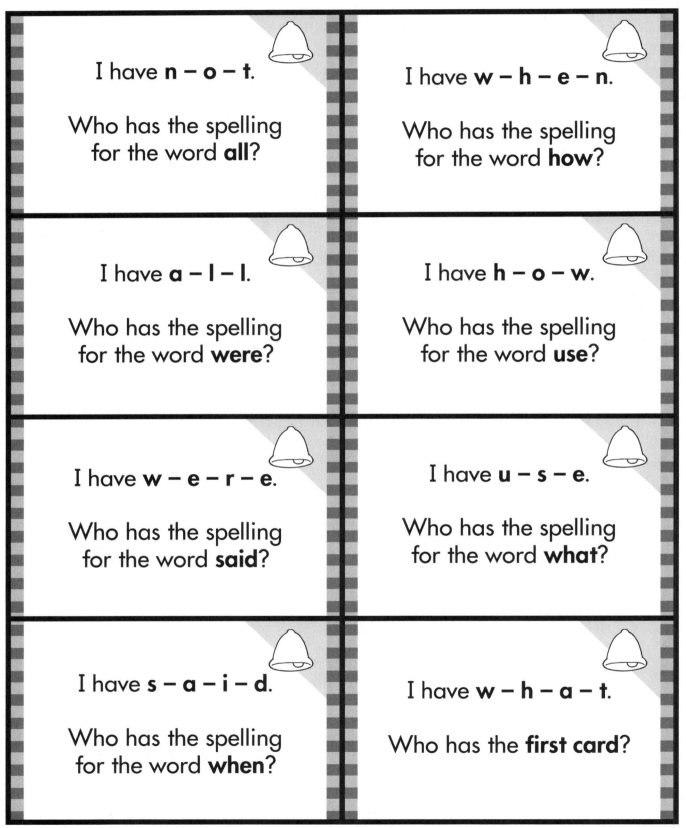

I have **n – o – t**.

Who has the spelling for the word **all**?

I have **w – h – e – n**.

Who has the spelling for the word **how**?

I have **a – l – l**.

Who has the spelling for the word **were**?

I have **h – o – w**.

Who has the spelling for the word **use**?

I have **w – e – r – e**.

Who has the spelling for the word **said**?

I have **u – s – e**.

Who has the spelling for the word **what**?

I have **s – a – i – d**.

Who has the spelling for the word **when**?

I have **w – h – a – t**.

Who has the **first card**?

I Have, Who Has?: Language Arts • 1–2 © 2007 Creative Teaching Press

Name _____ Date _____

Spelling 1

I Write the spelling of each word as it is said. Write words from left to right.

→			

II Choose four of the words from the table. Write each word four times.

1. _____ _____ _____ _____

2. _____ _____ _____ _____

3. _____ _____ _____ _____

4. _____ _____ _____ _____

Spelling 2

I have the **first card**.

Who has the spelling for the word **like**?

I have **s – o – m – e**.

Who has the spelling for the word **them**?

I have **l – i – k – e**.

Who has the spelling for the word **many**?

I have **t – h – e – m**.

Who has the spelling for the word **make**?

I have **m – a – n – y**.

Who has the spelling for the word **then**?

I have **m – a – k – e**.

Who has the spelling for the word **about**?

I have **t – h – e – n**.

Who has the spelling for the word **some**?

I have **a – b – o – u – t**.

Who has the spelling for the word **look**?

I Have, Who Has?: Language Arts • 1–2 © 2007 Creative Teaching Press

Spelling 2

I have **l – o – o – k**.

Who has the spelling for the word **out**?

I have **i – n – t – o**.

Who has the spelling for the word **has**?

I have **o – u – t**.

Who has the spelling for the word **more**?

I have **h – a – s**.

Who has the spelling for the word **him**?

I have **m – o – r – e**.

Who has the spelling for the word **see**?

I have **h – i – m**.

Who has the spelling for the word **her**?

I have **s – e – e**.

Who has the spelling for the word **into**?

I have **h – e – r**.

Who has the spelling for the word **way**?

I Have, Who Has?: Language Arts • 1–2 © 2007 Creative Teaching Press

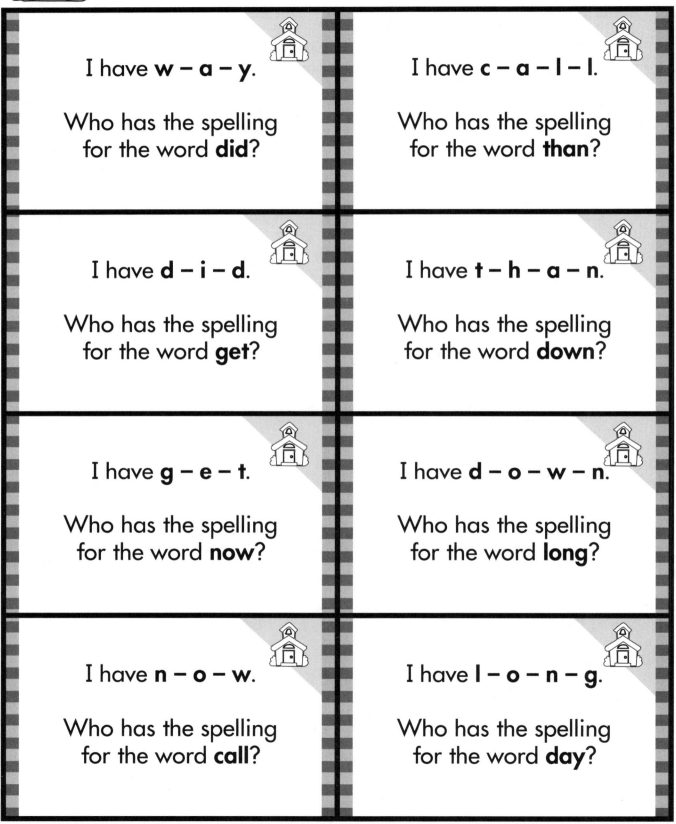

I have **w – a – y**.

Who has the spelling for the word **did**?

I have **c – a – l – l**.

Who has the spelling for the word **than**?

I have **d – i – d**.

Who has the spelling for the word **get**?

I have **t – h – a – n**.

Who has the spelling for the word **down**?

I have **g – e – t**.

Who has the spelling for the word **now**?

I have **d – o – w – n**.

Who has the spelling for the word **long**?

I have **n – o – w**.

Who has the spelling for the word **call**?

I have **l – o – n – g**.

Who has the spelling for the word **day**?

I Have, Who Has?: Language Arts • 1–2 © 2007 Creative Teaching Press

Spelling 2

I have **d – a – y**.

Who has the spelling for the word **find**?

I have **w – o – u – l – d**.

Who has the spelling for the word **other**?

I have **f – i – n – d**.

Who has the spelling for the word **these**?

I have **o – t – h – e – r**.

Who has the spelling for the word **take**?

I have **t – h – e – s – e**.

Who has the spelling for the word **could**?

I have **t – a – k – e**.

Who has the spelling for the word **over**?

I have **c – o – u – l – d**.

Who has the spelling for the word **would**?

I have **o – v – e – r**.

Who has the **first card**?

I Have, Who Has? Language Arts • 1–2 © 2007 Creative Teaching Press

Name _____ Date _____

Spelling 2

I Write the spelling of each word as it is said. Write words from left to right.

→			

II Choose four of the words from the table. Write each word four times.

1._____ _____ _____ _____

2._____ _____ _____ _____

3._____ _____ _____ _____

4._____ _____ _____ _____

I Have, Who Has?: Language Arts • 1–2 © 2007 Creative Teaching Press

Common Nouns

I have the **first card**.

Who has the common
noun in this sentence?
I like my dog.

I have **rat**.

Who has the common
noun in this sentence?
I can see the bike.

I have **dog**.

Who has the common
noun in this sentence?
I see a rainbow.

I have **bike**.

Who has the common
noun in this sentence?
I ran to the store.

I have **rainbow**.

Who has the common
noun in this sentence?
I made a cake.

I have **store**.

Who has the common
noun in this sentence?
I will go to the park.

I have **cake**.

Who has the common
noun in this sentence?
I saw a rat.

I have **park**.

Who has the common
noun in this sentence?
I like to watch the birds.

Common Nouns

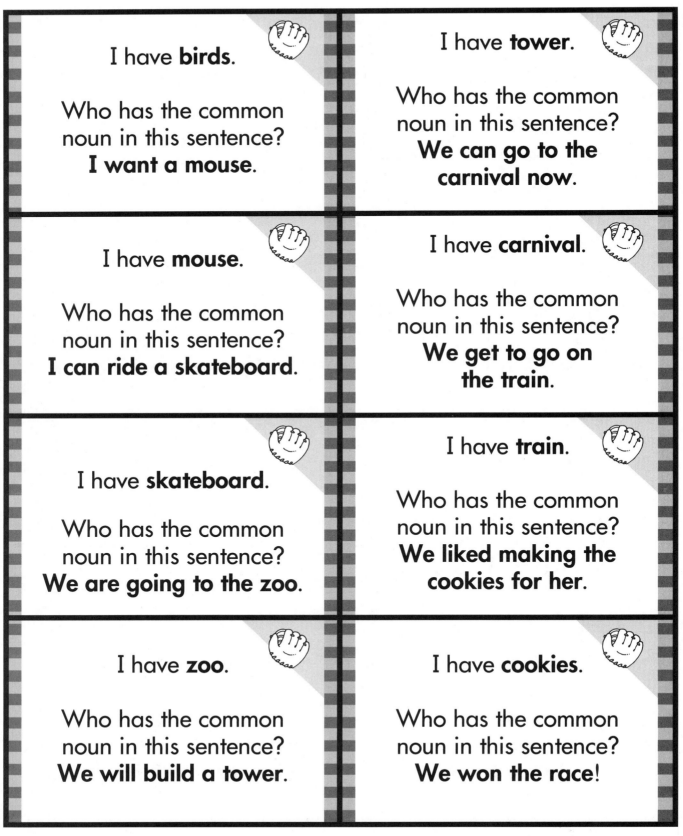

I have **birds**.

Who has the common noun in this sentence? **I want a mouse**.

I have **tower**.

Who has the common noun in this sentence? **We can go to the carnival now**.

I have **mouse**.

Who has the common noun in this sentence? **I can ride a skateboard**.

I have **carnival**.

Who has the common noun in this sentence? **We get to go on the train**.

I have **skateboard**.

Who has the common noun in this sentence? **We are going to the zoo**.

I have **train**.

Who has the common noun in this sentence? **We liked making the cookies for her**.

I have **zoo**.

Who has the common noun in this sentence? **We will build a tower**.

I have **cookies**.

Who has the common noun in this sentence? **We won the race!**

I Have, Who Has?: Language Arts • 1–2 © 2007 Creative Teaching Press

Common Nouns

I have **race**.

Who has the common noun in this sentence? **We are out of peanut butter today**.

I have **pool**.

Who has the common noun in this sentence? **Do you know how to make a milkshake?**

I have **peanut butter**.

Who has the common noun in this sentence? **We played at her house**.

I have **milkshake**.

Who has the common noun in this sentence? **Do you know who bought the new car?**

I have **house**.

Who has the common noun in this sentence? **We want to go see a movie tonight**.

I have **car**.

Who has the common noun in this sentence? **Do you see my keys anywhere?**

I have **movie**.

Who has the common noun in this sentence? **Do you want to swim in my pool?**

I have **keys**.

Who has the common noun in this sentence? **Do you plan to move close to the beach?**

I Have, Who Has? Language Arts • 1–2 © 2007 Creative Teaching Press

Common Nouns

I have **beach**.

Who has the common noun in this sentence? **Where are my new shoes hiding?**

I have **book**.

Who has the common noun in this sentence? **Did you say you wanted a bunny?**

I have **shoes**.

Who has the common noun in this sentence? **Where is her new office?**

I have **bunny**.

Who has the common noun in this sentence? **Have you seen her new dress?**

I have **office**.

Who has the common noun in this sentence? **Did you finish your homework?**

I have **dress**.

Who has the common noun in this sentence? **Do you know where I left my sunglasses?**

I have **homework**.

Who has the common noun in this sentence? **Did you read the book to her?**

I have **sunglasses**.

Who has the **first card**?

Name _____ Date _____

Common Nouns

I Follow the path by coloring the common nouns as your classmates name them.

*Start	park	birds	mouse
dog	store	zoo	skateboard
rainbow	bike	tower	carnival
cake	rat	cookies	train
house	peanut butter	race	It's
movie	your	shoes	office
pool	keys	beach	homework
milkshake	car	name	book
*Finish	sunglasses	dress	bunny

II **Riddle: What belongs to you but other people use it more than you do?**

Write the words left over on the lines below to answer the riddle.

Solution: _____ _____ _____.

Which word in the solution above is the common noun? _____

Proper Nouns

I have the **first card**.

Who has the proper noun in this sentence? **Where did Mary go?**

I have **Mexico**.

Who has the proper noun in this sentence? **Can I borrow your book called <u>Riddle</u> <u>Me</u>?**

I have **Mary**.

Who has the proper noun in this sentence? **I am going to the zoo with Linda.**

I have **<u>Riddle</u> <u>Me</u>**.

Who has the proper noun in this sentence? **She ordered her new wood floor from Drake's Carpet.**

I have **Linda**.

Who has the proper noun in this sentence? **Are you ready to go shopping at MiniMart?**

I have **Drake's Carpet**.

Who has the proper noun in this sentence? **He named his new puppy Shasta.**

I have **MiniMart**.

Who has the proper noun in this sentence? **We will leave for Mexico in two days.**

I have **Shasta**.

Who has the proper noun in this sentence? **We are eating dinner with Tom.**

I Have, Who Has?: Language Arts • 1–2 © 2007 Creative Teaching Press

Proper Nouns

I have **Tom**.

Who has the proper noun in this sentence? **Have you ever been to Texas?**

I have **Wednesday**.

Who has the proper noun in this sentence? **Did you know that my birthday is in May?**

I have **Texas**.

Who has the proper noun in this sentence? **Do you want a bite of my cookie from B. B.'s Bakery?**

I have **May**.

Who has the proper noun in this sentence? **She starts kindergarten at Weaver Elementary next week.**

I have **B. B.'s Bakery**.

Who has the proper noun in this sentence? **Donna sold the house across the street.**

I have **Weaver Elementary**.

Who has the proper noun in this sentence? **Mario won $100.00 in the contest.**

I have **Donna**.

Who has the proper noun in this sentence? **Did you go to the concert last Wednesday night?**

I have **Mario**.

Who has the proper noun in this sentence? **Last Sunday, we went to the carnival.**

Proper Nouns

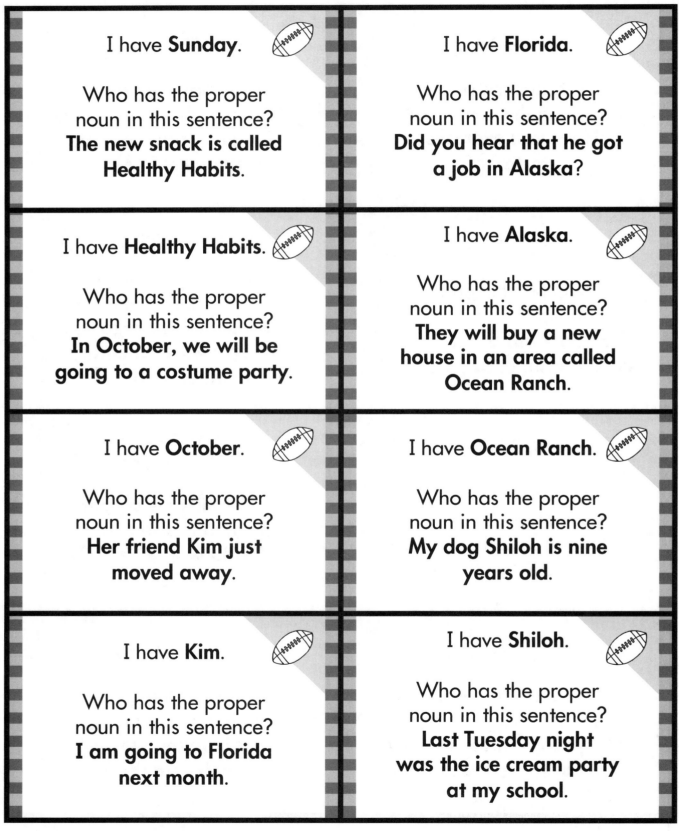

I have **Sunday**.

Who has the proper noun in this sentence? **The new snack is called Healthy Habits.**

I have **Florida**.

Who has the proper noun in this sentence? **Did you hear that he got a job in Alaska?**

I have **Healthy Habits**.

Who has the proper noun in this sentence? **In October, we will be going to a costume party.**

I have **Alaska**.

Who has the proper noun in this sentence? **They will buy a new house in an area called Ocean Ranch.**

I have **October**.

Who has the proper noun in this sentence? **Her friend Kim just moved away.**

I have **Ocean Ranch**.

Who has the proper noun in this sentence? **My dog Shiloh is nine years old.**

I have **Kim**.

Who has the proper noun in this sentence? **I am going to Florida next month.**

I have **Shiloh**.

Who has the proper noun in this sentence? **Last Tuesday night was the ice cream party at my school.**

I Have, Who Has?: Language Arts • 1–2 © 2007 Creative Teaching Press

Proper Nouns

I have **Tuesday**.

Who has the proper noun in this sentence? **Did you hear that Brenton is getting a hearing aid?**

I have **Paul**.

Who has the proper noun in this sentence? **Do you want to go with me to Skate Depot?**

I have **Brenton**.

Who has the proper noun in this sentence? **She works for the MIND Institute.**

I have **Skate Depot**.

Who has the proper noun in this sentence? **He just opened his first shop, Full Motorsports.**

I have **MIND Institute**.

Who has the proper noun in this sentence? **They are taking their boat to Lake Superior.**

I have **Full Motorsports**.

Who has the proper noun in this sentence? **Her sister just moved to Kentucky.**

I have **Lake Superior**.

Who has the proper noun in this sentence? **Have you seen Paul lately?**

I have **Kentucky**.

Who has the **first card**?

Proper Nouns

I Follow the path by coloring the proper nouns as your classmates name them.

*Start	The	Drake's Carpet	Shasta
Mary	Mexico	Riddle Me	Tom
Linda	MiniMart	African	Texas
May	Wednesday	Donna	B. B.'s Bakery
Weaver Elementary	Mario	Sunday	Healthy Habits
Shiloh	Ocean Ranch	Kim	October
Tuesday	Alaska	Florida	elephants
Brenton	Paul	Skate Depot	*Finish
MIND Institute	Lake Superior	Full Motorsports	Kentucky

II **Fun Fact: What animals flap their large ears to keep themselves cool in Africa?**

Write the words left over in order on the lines below to answer the Fun Fact question.

Solution: _____ _____ _____ .

Which word in the solution above is the proper noun? _____

I Have, Who Has?: Language Arts • 1–2 © 2007 Creative Teaching Press

Action Verbs

I have the **first card**.

Who has the action verb
in this sentence?
I ran to the corner.

I have **flew**.

Who has the action verb
in this sentence?
**The rat chewed a hole
in her coat**.

I have **ran**.

Who has the action verb
in this sentence?
She bit into the apple.

I have **chewed**.

Who has the action verb
in this sentence?
**The repairman fixed
her sink**.

I have **bit**.

Who has the action verb
in this sentence?
**He blew a bubble with
his gum**.

I have **fixed**.

Who has the action verb
in this sentence?
**His new car drove
for miles**.

I have **blew**.

Who has the action verb
in this sentence?
**The plane flew to
California**.

I have **drove**.

Who has the action verb
in this sentence?
They won the contest.

Action Verbs

I have **won**.

Who has the action verb
in this sentence?
**The crowd cheered
for the home team.**

I have **read**.

Who has the action verb
in this sentence?
**She dreamed of animals
every night.**

I have **cheered**.

Who has the action verb
in this sentence?
**Where did you hide
that present?**

I have **dreamed**.

Who has the action verb
in this sentence?
**The mother bird fed
her baby birds.**

I have **hide**.

Who has the action verb
in this sentence?
**She sold the books
at an auction.**

I have **fed**.

Who has the action verb
in this sentence?
**She gave the man
five dollars.**

I have **sold**.

Who has the action verb
in this sentence?
**He read the book
to his sister.**

I have **gave**.

Who has the action verb
in this sentence?
They left on the train.

I Have, Who Has?: Language Arts • 1–2 © 2007 Creative Teaching Press

Action Verbs

I have **left**.

Who has the action verb
in this sentence?
**They will sell their table
next week**.

I have **heard**.

Who has the action verb
in this sentence?
The pitcher threw the ball.

I have **sell**.

Who has the action verb
in this sentence?
**The bee stung her
on the hand**.

I have **threw**.

Who has the action verb
in this sentence?
**She dialed the number
on the phone**.

I have **stung**.

Who has the action verb
in this sentence?
**They worked hard
in the yard**.

I have **dialed**.

Who has the action verb
in this sentence?
**Keith opened the door
for his friend**.

I have **worked**.

Who has the action verb
in this sentence?
They heard an odd noise.

I have **opened**.

Who has the action verb
in this sentence?
**They bought some bagels
at the bakery**.

I Have, Who Has?: Language Arts • 1–2 © 2007 Creative Teaching Press

Action Verbs

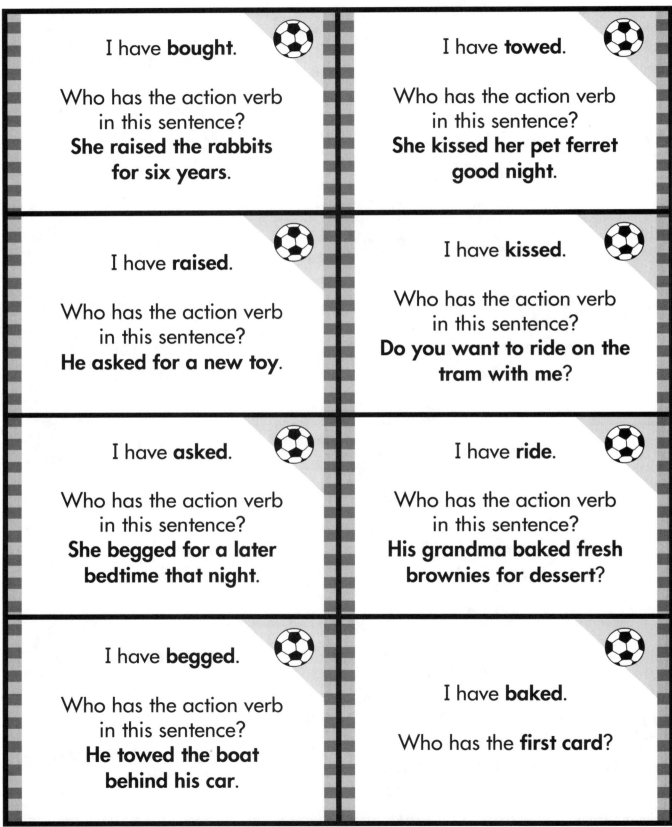

I have **bought**.

Who has the action verb
in this sentence?
**She raised the rabbits
for six years.**

I have **towed**.

Who has the action verb
in this sentence?
**She kissed her pet ferret
good night.**

I have **raised**.

Who has the action verb
in this sentence?
He asked for a new toy.

I have **kissed**.

Who has the action verb
in this sentence?
**Do you want to ride on the
tram with me?**

I have **asked**.

Who has the action verb
in this sentence?
**She begged for a later
bedtime that night.**

I have **ride**.

Who has the action verb
in this sentence?
**His grandma baked fresh
brownies for dessert?**

I have **begged**.

Who has the action verb
in this sentence?
**He towed the boat
behind his car.**

I have **baked**.

Who has the **first card**?

I Have, Who Has?: Language Arts • 1–2 © 2007 Creative Teaching Press

Name _____ Date _____

Action Verbs

I Follow the path by coloring the action verbs as your classmates name them.

*Start	ran	bit	blew
sold	hide	sleep	flew
read	cheered	won	chewed
dreamed	fed	drove	fixed
three	gave	left	sell
threw	heard	worked	stung
dialed	raised	asked	begged
opened	bought	kissed	towed
*Finish	baked	ride	years

II Fun Fact: How long can snails sleep?

Write the words left over on the lines below to answer the Fun Fact question.

Solution: <u>Snails</u>   <u>can</u>   _____ _____ _____.

Which word in the solution is the action verb? _____

I Have, Who Has?: Language Arts • 1–2 © 2007 Creative Teaching Press

Verb Tenses

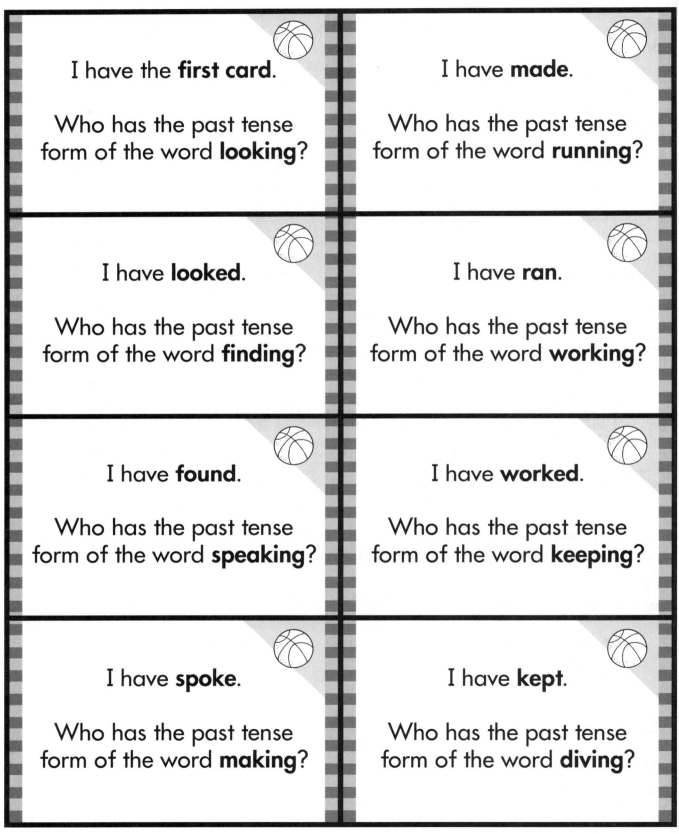

I have the **first card**.

Who has the past tense form of the word **looking**?

I have **made**.

Who has the past tense form of the word **running**?

I have **looked**.

Who has the past tense form of the word **finding**?

I have **ran**.

Who has the past tense form of the word **working**?

I have **found**.

Who has the past tense form of the word **speaking**?

I have **worked**.

Who has the past tense form of the word **keeping**?

I have **spoke**.

Who has the past tense form of the word **making**?

I have **kept**.

Who has the past tense form of the word **diving**?

I Have, Who Has?: Language Arts • 1–2 © 2007 Creative Teaching Press

Verb Tenses

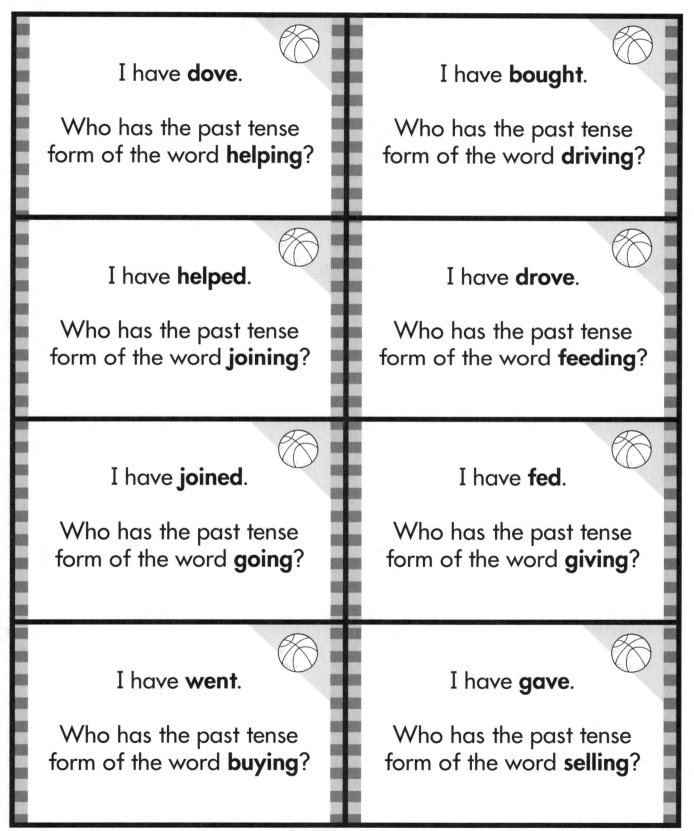

I have **dove**.

Who has the past tense form of the word **helping**?

I have **bought**.

Who has the past tense form of the word **driving**?

I have **helped**.

Who has the past tense form of the word **joining**?

I have **drove**.

Who has the past tense form of the word **feeding**?

I have **joined**.

Who has the past tense form of the word **going**?

I have **fed**.

Who has the past tense form of the word **giving**?

I have **went**.

Who has the past tense form of the word **buying**?

I have **gave**.

Who has the past tense form of the word **selling**?

I Have, Who Has?: Language Arts • 1–2 © 2007 Creative Teaching Press

Verb Tenses

I have **sold**.

Who has the past tense form of the word **chewing**?

I have **drank**.

Who has the past tense form of the word **watching**?

I have **chewed**.

Who has the past tense form of the word **hiding**?

I have **watched**.

Who has the past tense form of the word **seeing**?

I have **hid**.

Who has the past tense form of the word **hearing**?

I have **saw**.

Who has the past tense form of the word **wanting**?

I have **heard**.

Who has the past tense form of the word **drinking**?

I have **wanted**.

Who has the past tense form of the word **putting**?

Verb Tenses

I have **put**.

Who has the past tense form of the word **doing**?

I have **said**.

Who has the past tense form of the word **baking**?

I have **did**.

Who has the past tense form of the word **calling**?

I have **baked**.

Who has the past tense form of the word **leaving**?

I have **called**.

Who has the past tense form of the word **taking**?

I have **left**.

Who has the past tense form of the word **holding**?

I have **took**.

Who has the past tense form of the word **saying**?

I have **held**.

Who has the **first card**?

Verb Tenses

I Follow the path by coloring the past tense verbs as your classmates name them.

*Start	looked	dove	helped
spoke	found	kept	joined
made	ran	worked	went
chewed	sold	Stick	bought
hid	gave	fed	drove
heard	out	wanted	put
drank	watched	saw	did
held	left	tongue	called
*Finish	baked	said	took

 II **Fun Fact: What can you do that a crocodile cannot?**

Write the words left over on the lines below to answer the Fun Fact question.

Solution: _____ _____ **your** _____ .

(but you shouldn't)

Which word in the solution above is the present tense verb? _____

What is that word in the past tense? _____

I Have, Who Has?: Language Arts • 1–2 © 2007 Creative Teaching Press

Adjectives 1

I have the **first card**.

Who has the adjective
in this sentence?
I ate a hot sandwich.

I have **round**.

Who has the adjective
in this sentence?
**That lazy pig on the farm
loves the mud.**

I have **hot**.

Who has the adjective
in this sentence?
**Did you see that
big butterfly?**

I have **lazy**.

Who has the adjective
in this sentence?
**The green frog was
hopping in front of me.**

I have **big**.

Who has the adjective
in this sentence?
The sun is so bright today.

I have **green**.

Who has the adjective
in this sentence?
It's such a cold day today.

I have **bright**.

Who has the adjective
in this sentence?
**There is a round chair
in the corner.**

I have **cold**.

Who has the adjective
in this sentence?
Your dress is so colorful.

Adjectives 1

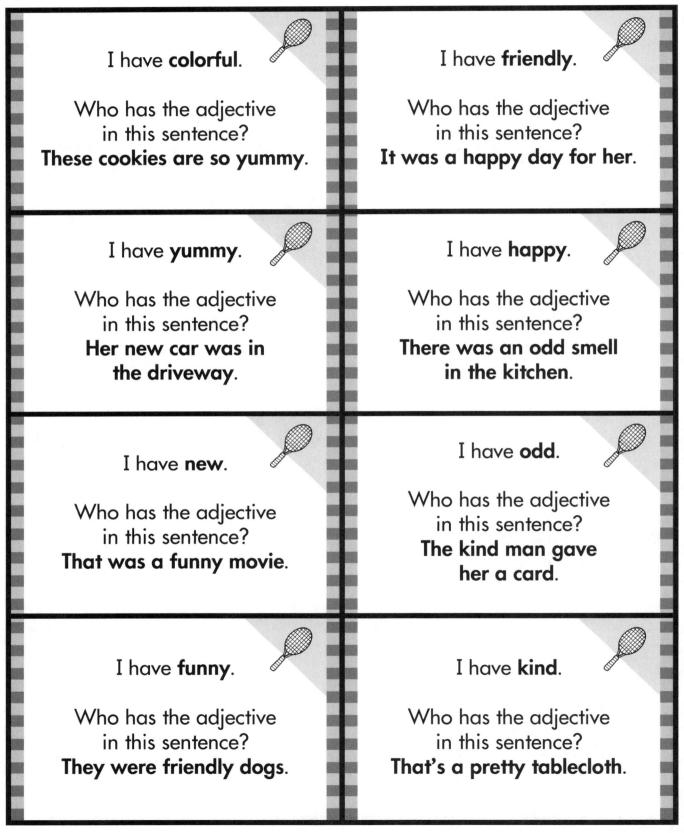

I have **colorful**.

Who has the adjective in this sentence?
These cookies are so yummy.

I have **friendly**.

Who has the adjective in this sentence?
It was a happy day for her.

I have **yummy**.

Who has the adjective in this sentence?
Her new car was in the driveway.

I have **happy**.

Who has the adjective in this sentence?
There was an odd smell in the kitchen.

I have **new**.

Who has the adjective in this sentence?
That was a funny movie.

I have **odd**.

Who has the adjective in this sentence?
The kind man gave her a card.

I have **funny**.

Who has the adjective in this sentence?
They were friendly dogs.

I have **kind**.

Who has the adjective in this sentence?
That's a pretty tablecloth.

I Have, Who Has?: Language Arts • 1–2 © 2007 Creative Teaching Press

Adjectives 1

I have **pretty**.

Who has the adjective
in this sentence?
**There are free tickets
in the mail.**

I have **dirty**.

Who has the adjective
in this sentence?
**The dishes were cheap
at the sale.**

I have **free**.

Who has the adjective
in this sentence?
**The hollow tree was the
squirrel's home.**

I have **cheap**.

Who has the adjective
in this sentence?
**The loud noises wake
her up at night.**

I have **hollow**.

Who has the adjective
in this sentence?
**It was a dark night in
the woods.**

I have **loud**.

Who has the adjective
in this sentence?
**There were different
toppings for the ice cream.**

I have **dark**.

Who has the adjective
in this sentence?
Her room was so dirty!

I have **different**.

Who has the adjective
in this sentence?
**He liked watching the
calm waves of the ocean.**

Adjectives 1

I have **calm**.

Who has the adjective
in this sentence?
**Her loving class gave
her hugs.**

I have **scary**.

Who has the adjective
in this sentence?
**It was a long drive to
the country.**

I have **loving**.

Who has the adjective
in this sentence?
**They got lost in the
crowded city.**

I have **long**.

Who has the adjective
in this sentence?
**Her curly hair blew
in the wind.**

I have **crowded**.

Who has the adjective
in this sentence?
**She walked through the
open door.**

I have **curly**.

Who has the adjective
in this sentence?
**The empty bottle was put
into the basket.**

I have **open**.

Who has the adjective
in this sentence?
They saw a scary movie.

I have **empty**.

Who has the **first card**?

I Have, Who Has?: Language Arts • 1–2 © 2007 Creative Teaching Press

Name _____ Date _____

Adjectives 1

I Follow the path by coloring the adjectives as your classmates name them.

hot	***Start**				***Finish**
big	open	scary	long	curly	empty
bright	crowded	loving	calm	different	loud
round	free	hollow	dark	dirty	cheap
lazy	pretty	kind	odd	happy	friendly
green	cold	colorful	yummy	new	funny
A	**B**	**C**	**D**	**E**	**F**

II Write your favorite adjective in the blank box above.

III Circle three adjectives from Column C.
Write a sentence for each. Then draw a line under the adjective.

1. _____

2. _____

3. _____

Adjectives 2

I have the **first card**.

Who has the adjective in this sentence?
She had a big dinosaur on her cake.

I have **tiny**.

Who has the adjective in this sentence?
It was a quiet day in the classroom.

I have **big**.

Who has the adjective in this sentence?
The boiling water is for making tea.

I have **quiet**.

Who has the adjective in this sentence?
The purring cat was resting.

I have **boiling**.

Who has the adjective in this sentence?
The chubby baby was smiling.

I have **purring**.

Who has the adjective in this sentence?
I like the many colors in the painting.

I have **chubby**.

Who has the adjective in this sentence?
He saw a tiny mouse run by his feet.

I have **many**.

Who has the adjective in this sentence?
The small chair was just her size.

Adjectives 2

I have **small**.

Who has the adjective
in this sentence?
**She liked lying on a raft in
the shallow water.**

I have **enormous**.

Who has the adjective
in this sentence?
The baby had such soft hair.

I have **shallow**.

Who has the adjectives
in this sentence?
**They were going to the
antique car show.**

I have **soft**.

Who has the adjective
in this sentence?
**The sticky jam was all
over the counter.**

I have **antique** and **car**.

Who has the adjective
in this sentence?
**Why is that noisy group
still outside?**

I have **sticky**.

Who has the adjective
in this sentence?
**She hung the damp towel
out to dry.**

I have **noisy**.

Who has the adjective
in this sentence?
**The waiter brought out an
enormous bowl of pasta.**

I have **damp**.

Who has the adjective
in this sentence?
**There was a straight path
to the garden.**

Adjectives 2

I have **straight**.

Who has the adjective in this sentence?
The fluffy cat just came from the groomer.

I have **thick**.

Who has the adjective in this sentence?
Her feet were filthy from playing in the mud.

I have **fluffy**.

Who has the adjective in this sentence?
The young boy loved to sleep late.

I have **filthy**.

Who has the adjective in this sentence?
He was such a helpful boy.

I have **young**.

Who has the adjective in this sentence?
The fast car won the race.

I have **helpful**.

Who has the adjective in this sentence?
Are you a respectful class?

I have **fast**.

Who has the adjective in this sentence?
It was hard to walk through the thick brush.

I have **respectful**.

Who has the adjective in this sentence?
The popular show was sold out.

I Have, Who Has?: Language Arts • 1–2 © 2007 Creative Teaching Press

Adjectives 2

I have **popular**.

Who has the adjective in this sentence? **She almost slipped on the wet floor**.

I have **wise**.

Who has the adjective in this sentence? **She was the first person to earn a trophy**.

I have **wet**.

Who has the adjective in this sentence? **The smart boy went to college**.

I have **first**.

Who has the adjective in this sentence? **Lynn wanted a secret room built in her house**.

I have **smart**.

Who has the adjective in this sentence? **The exciting movie was packed with people**.

I have **secret**.

Who has the adjective in this sentence? **Did you see her six ducklings**?

I have **exciting**.

Who has the adjective in this sentence? **You might see a wise owl in a cartoon**.

I have **six**.

Who has the **first card**?

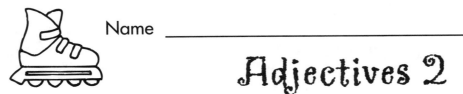

Name _____   Date _____

Adjectives 2

I Follow the path by coloring the adjectives as your classmates name them.

*Start	big	boiling	chubby	purring	many
damp	sticky	soft	tiny	quiet	small
straight	fluffy	enormous	noisy	antique, car	shallow
fast	young	wet	smart	first	secret
thick	respectful	popular	exciting	wise	six
filthy	helpful				*Finish

II Write your favorite adjective in the blank box above.

III Which adjective from the table above best describes each noun below?
Write it.

1. _____ pudding

2. _____ towels

3. _____ friend

4. _____ car

5. _____ hen house

6. _____ line

Basic Vocabulary Development

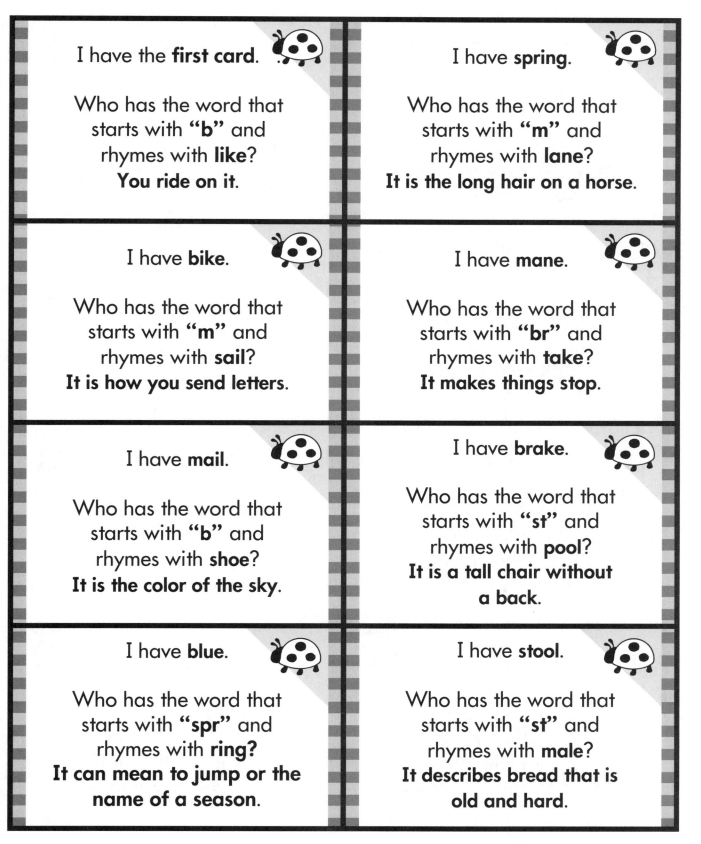

I have the **first card.**

Who has the word that starts with **"b"** and rhymes with **like**? **You ride on it.**

I have **spring.**

Who has the word that starts with **"m"** and rhymes with **lane**? **It is the long hair on a horse.**

I have **bike.**

Who has the word that starts with **"m"** and rhymes with **sail**? **It is how you send letters.**

I have **mane.**

Who has the word that starts with **"br"** and rhymes with **take**? **It makes things stop.**

I have **mail.**

Who has the word that starts with **"b"** and rhymes with **shoe**? **It is the color of the sky.**

I have **brake.**

Who has the word that starts with **"st"** and rhymes with **pool**? **It is a tall chair without a back.**

I have **blue.**

Who has the word that starts with **"spr"** and rhymes with **ring**? **It can mean to jump or the name of a season.**

I have **stool.**

Who has the word that starts with **"st"** and rhymes with **male**? **It describes bread that is old and hard.**

Basic Vocabulary Development

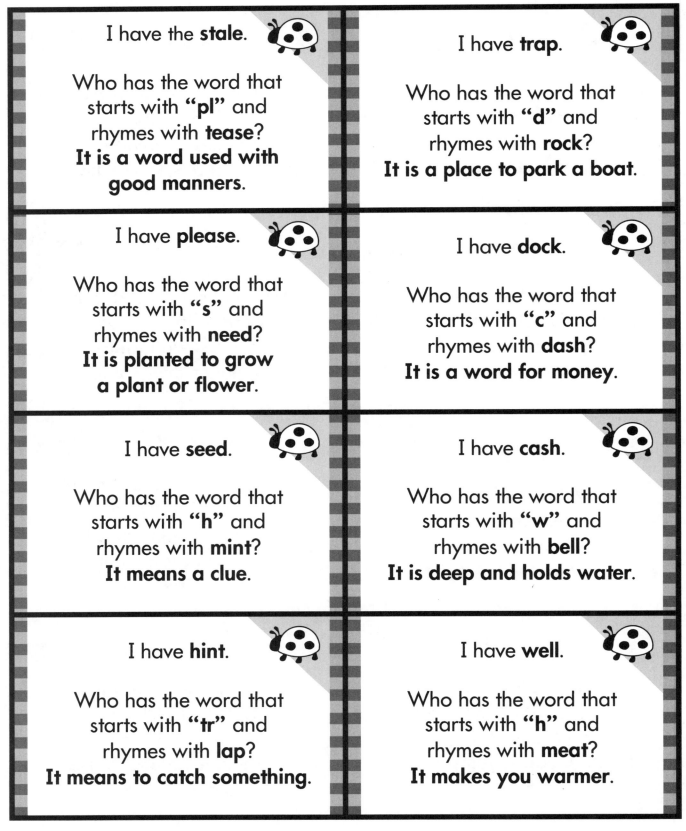

I have the **stale**.

Who has the word that starts with **"pl"** and rhymes with **tease**? **It is a word used with good manners.**

I have **trap**.

Who has the word that starts with **"d"** and rhymes with **rock**? **It is a place to park a boat.**

I have **please**.

Who has the word that starts with **"s"** and rhymes with **need**? **It is planted to grow a plant or flower.**

I have **dock**.

Who has the word that starts with **"c"** and rhymes with **dash**? **It is a word for money.**

I have **seed**.

Who has the word that starts with **"h"** and rhymes with **mint**? **It means a clue.**

I have **cash**.

Who has the word that starts with **"w"** and rhymes with **bell**? **It is deep and holds water.**

I have **hint**.

Who has the word that starts with **"tr"** and rhymes with **lap**? **It means to catch something.**

I have **well**.

Who has the word that starts with **"h"** and rhymes with **meat**? **It makes you warmer.**

I Have, Who Has?: Language Arts • 1–2 © 2007 Creative Teaching Press

Basic Vocabulary Development

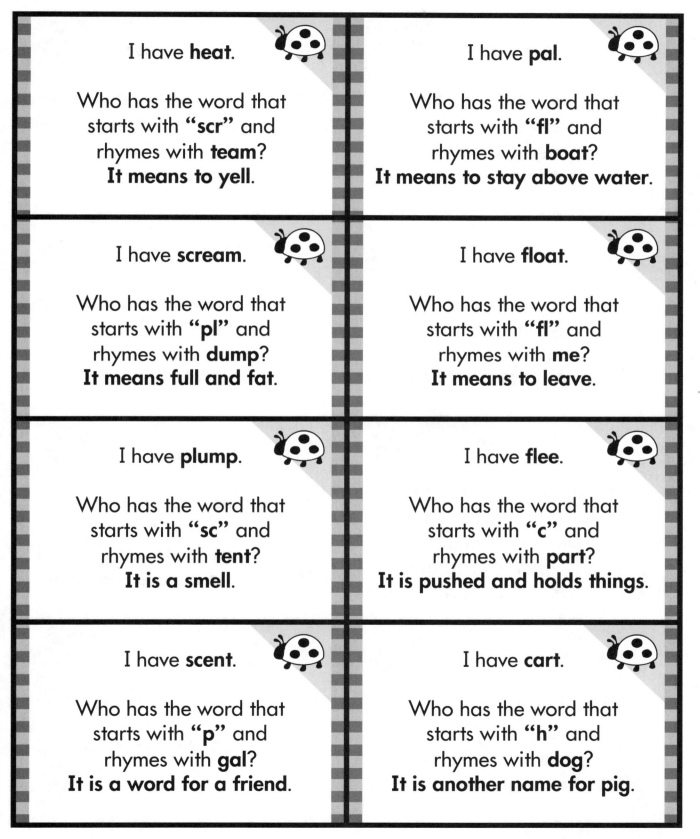

I have **heat**.

Who has the word that starts with **"scr"** and rhymes with **team**? **It means to yell**.

I have **pal**.

Who has the word that starts with **"fl"** and rhymes with **boat**? **It means to stay above water**.

I have **scream**.

Who has the word that starts with **"pl"** and rhymes with **dump**? **It means full and fat**.

I have **float**.

Who has the word that starts with **"fl"** and rhymes with **me**? **It means to leave**.

I have **plump**.

Who has the word that starts with **"sc"** and rhymes with **tent**? **It is a smell**.

I have **flee**.

Who has the word that starts with **"c"** and rhymes with **part**? **It is pushed and holds things**.

I have **scent**.

Who has the word that starts with **"p"** and rhymes with **gal**? **It is a word for a friend**.

I have **cart**.

Who has the word that starts with **"h"** and rhymes with **dog**? **It is another name for pig**.

Basic Vocabulary Development

I have **hog**.

Who has the word that starts with "**m**" and rhymes with **hair**?
It is a female horse.

I have **geese**.

Who has the word that starts with "**thr**" and rhymes with **bone**?
It is where a king sits.

I have **mare**.

Who has the word that starts with "**st**" and rhymes with **eye**.
It is a pig's messy home.

I have **throne**.

Who has the word that starts with "**fl**" and rhymes with **trip**?
It means to turn over.

I have **sty**.

Who has the word that starts with "**cr**" and rhymes with **dime**?
It is when someone breaks the law.

I have **flip**.

Who has the word that starts with "**tr**" and rhymes with **must**?
It means to believe someone.

I have **crime**.

Who has the word that starts with "**g**" and rhymes with **peace**?
It is more than one goose.

I have **trust**.

Who has the **first card**?

I Have, Who Has?: Language Arts • 1–2 © 2007 Creative Teaching Press

Name _____ Date _____

Basic Vocabulary Development

I Follow the path by coloring the words as your classmates name them.

*Start	bike	heat	scream	plump	scent
blue	mail	well	flee	float	pal
spring	mane	cash	cart	hog	mare
stool	brake	dock	trap	crime	sty
stale	please	seed	hint	geese	throne
			*Finish	trust	flip

II Write your favorite one-syllable word in the blank box above.

III Circle four words from the table above. Use each word in a complete sentence.

1. _____

2. _____

3. _____

4. _____

I Have, Who Has?: Language Arts • 1–2 © 2007 Creative Teaching Press

Advanced Vocabulary Development

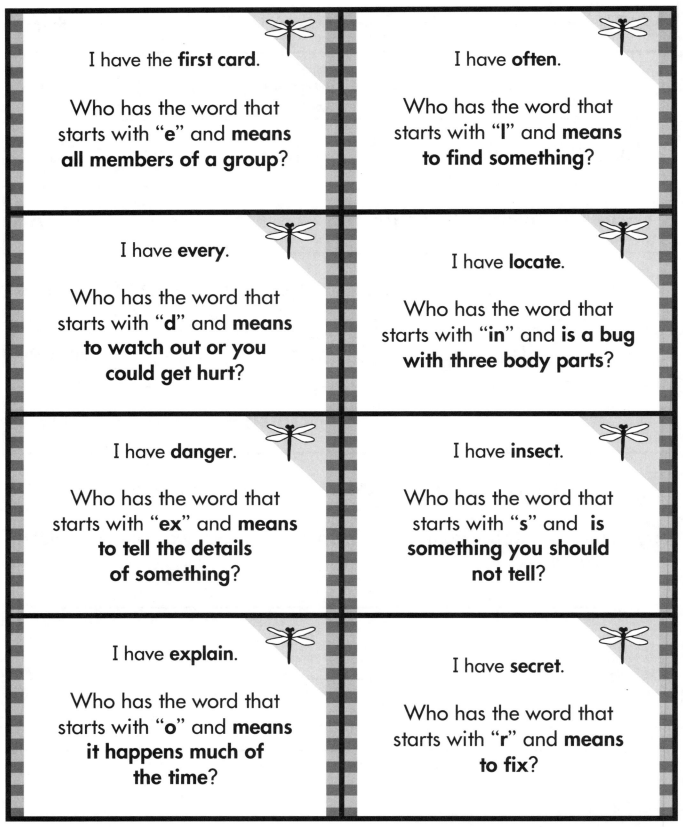

I have the **first card**.

Who has the word that starts with "**e**" and **means all members of a group**?

I have **often**.

Who has the word that starts with "**l**" and **means to find something**?

I have **every**.

Who has the word that starts with "**d**" and **means to watch out or you could get hurt**?

I have **locate**.

Who has the word that starts with "**in**" and **is a bug with three body parts**?

I have **danger**.

Who has the word that starts with "**ex**" and **means to tell the details of something**?

I have **insect**.

Who has the word that starts with "**s**" and **is something you should not tell**?

I have **explain**.

Who has the word that starts with "**o**" and **means it happens much of the time**?

I have **secret**.

Who has the word that starts with "**r**" and **means to fix**?

I Have, Who Has?: Language Arts • 1–2 © 2007 Creative Teaching Press

Advanced Vocabulary Development

I have **repair**.

Who has the word that starts with "**m**" and **is something a person does wrong**?

I have **combine**.

Who has the word that starts with "**d**" and **is a group of 12**?

I have **mistake**.

Who has the word that starts with "**t**" and **means late**?

I have **dozen**.

Who has the word that starts with "**s**" and **is when the sun goes down**?

I have **tardy**.

Who has the word that starts with "**a**" and **means to be scared**?

I have **sunset**.

Who has the word that starts with "**cr**" and **means to make**?

I have **afraid**.

Who has the word that starts with "**c**" and **means to join together**?

I have **create**.

Who has the word that starts with "**emp**" and **means there is nothing inside**?

Advanced Vocabulary Development

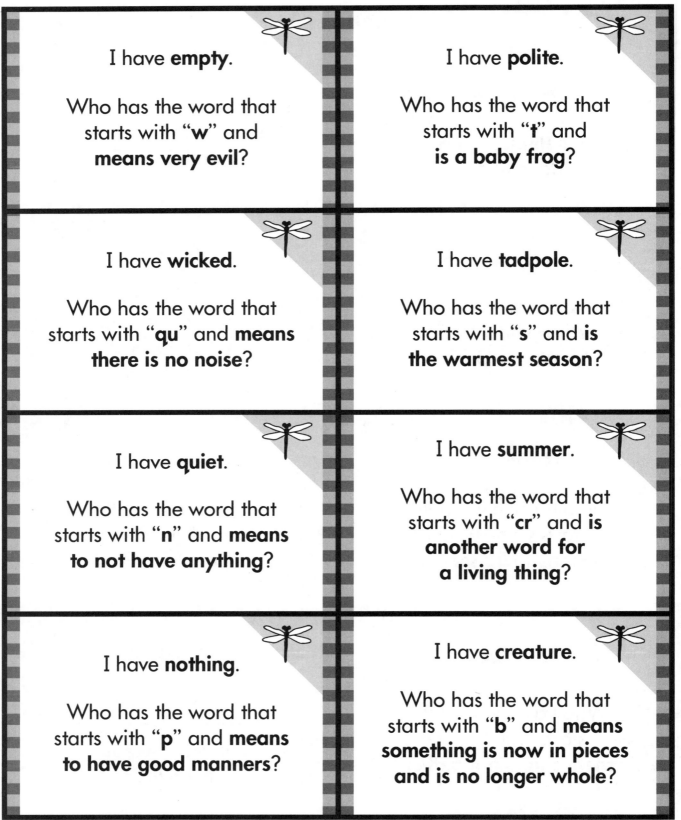

I have **empty**.

Who has the word that starts with "**w**" and **means very evil**?

I have **polite**.

Who has the word that starts with "**t**" and **is a baby frog**?

I have **wicked**.

Who has the word that starts with "**qu**" and **means there is no noise**?

I have **tadpole**.

Who has the word that starts with "**s**" and **is the warmest season**?

I have **quiet**.

Who has the word that starts with "**n**" and **means to not have anything**?

I have **summer**.

Who has the word that starts with "**cr**" and **is another word for a living thing**?

I have **nothing**.

Who has the word that starts with "**p**" and **means to have good manners**?

I have **creature**.

Who has the word that starts with "**b**" and **means something is now in pieces and is no longer whole**?

I Have, Who Has?: Language Arts • 1–2 © 2007 Creative Teaching Press

Advanced Vocabulary Development

I have **broken**.

Who has the word that starts with "**w**" and **is a person who brings food to a table**?

I have **quickly**.

Who has the word that starts with "**h**" and **is a word describing someone who tells the truth**?

I have **waiter**.

Who has the word that starts with "**st**" and **is a person you do not know and should not talk to**?

I have **honest**.

Who has the word that starts with "**h**" and **means 10 groups of 10**?

I have **stranger**.

Who has the word that starts with "**r**" and **means it is not fresh**?

I have **hundred**.

Who has the word that starts with "**s**" and **names a train that moves under the ground**?

I have **rotten**.

Who has the word that starts with "**qu**" and **means to do something very fast**?

I have **subway**.

Who has the **first card**?

Name _____ Date _____

Advanced Vocabulary Development

I Follow the path by coloring the words as your classmates name them.

*Start	secret	repair	mistake
every	insect	afraid	tardy
danger	locate	combine	dozen
explain	often	create	sunset
summer	tadpole	empty	wicked
creature	polite	nothing	quiet
broken	It's	hundred	subway
waiter	quickly	honest	*Finish
stranger	rotten	called	pod

II **Fun Fact: A group of lions is called a pride. What do you call a group of seals or whales?**

Write the words left over on the lines below to answer the Fun Fact question.

Solution: _____ _____ _____a_____ _____.

III Circle three words in the table above. Use each word in a complete sentence.

1. _____

2. _____

3. _____

I Have, Who Has?: Language Arts • 1–2 © 2007 Creative Teaching Press

Synonyms—Nouns

I have the **first card**.

Who has the synonym for **gift**?

I have **automobile**.

Who has the synonym for **illness**?

I have **present**.

Who has the synonym for **prize**?

I have **sickness**.

Who has the synonym for **baby**?

I have **reward**.

Who has the synonym for **scent**?

I have **infant**.

Who has the synonym for **idea**?

I have **smell**.

Who has the synonym for **car**?

I have **thought**.

Who has the synonym for **hat**?

Synonyms–Nouns

I have **cap**.

Who has the synonym
for **story**?

I have **rug**.

Who has the synonym
for **glue**?

I have **tale**.

Who has the synonym
for **dirt**?

I have **paste**.

Who has the synonym
for **ground**?

I have **soil**.

Who has the synonym
for **money**?

I have **floor**.

Who has the synonym
for **trip**?

I have **cash**.

Who has the synonym
for **carpet**?

I have **journey**.

Who has the synonym
for **lady**?

I Have, Who Has?: Language Arts • 1–2 © 2007 Creative Teaching Press

Synonyms—Nouns

I have **woman**.

Who has the synonym
for **child**?

I have **pair**.

Who has the synonym
for **trio**?

I have **youth**.

Who has the synonym
for **learner**?

I have **threesome**.

Who has the synonym
for **heat**?

I have **student**.

Who has the synonym
for **coach**?

I have **warmth**.

Who has the synonym
for **exercise**?

I have **trainer**.

Who has the synonym
for **couple**?

I have **workout**.

Who has the synonym
for **night**?

I Have, Who Has? Language Arts • 1–2 © 2007 Creative Teaching Press

Synonyms—Nouns

I have **evening**.

Who has the synonym for **price**?

I have **creature**.

Who has the synonym for **germ**?

I have **cost**.

Who has the synonym for **helper**?

I have **bug**.

Who has the synonym for **daybreak**?

I have **aide**.

Who has the synonym for a **place**?

I have **dawn**.

Who has the synonym for **trash**?

I have **spot**.

Who has the synonym for **animal**?

I have **garbage**.

Who has the **first card**?

I Have, Who Has?: Language Arts • 1–2 © 2007 Creative Teaching Press

Name _____ Date _____

Synonyms–Nouns

I Follow the path by coloring the nouns as your classmates name them.

*Start	present	reward	smell	automobile	sickness
cash	soil	tale	cap	thought	infant
rug	journey	woman	youth	student	trainer
paste	floor				pair
aide	cost	evening	workout	warmth	threesome
spot	creature	bug	dawn	garbage	*Finish
A	**B**	**C**	**D**	**E**	**F**

II Write your favorite pair of synonyms in the empty box above.

III Write a synonym for five of the nouns in Column B.

1. _____ is a synonym for _____

2. _____ is a synonym for _____

3. _____ is a synonym for _____

4. _____ is a synonym for _____

5. _____ is a synonym for _____

Synonyms—Verbs

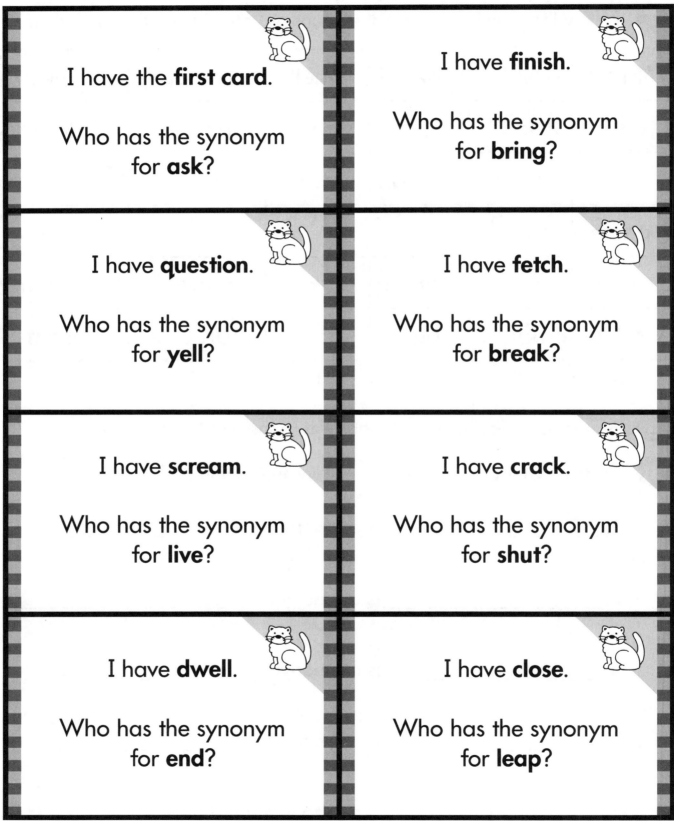

I have the **first card**.

Who has the synonym for **ask**?

I have **finish**.

Who has the synonym for **bring**?

I have **question**.

Who has the synonym for **yell**?

I have **fetch**.

Who has the synonym for **break**?

I have **scream**.

Who has the synonym for **live**?

I have **crack**.

Who has the synonym for **shut**?

I have **dwell**.

Who has the synonym for **end**?

I have **close**.

Who has the synonym for **leap**?

I Have, Who Has?: Language Arts • 1–2 © 2007 Creative Teaching Press

Synonyms—Verbs

I have **jump**.

Who has the synonym
for **heal**?

I have **open**.

Who has the synonym
for **forgive**?

I have **cure**.

Who has the synonym
for **leave**?

I have **excuse**.

Who has the synonym
for **keep**?

I have **go**.

Who has the synonym
for **have**?

I have **hold**.

Who has the synonym
for **fly**?

I have **own**.

Who has the synonym
for **unlock**?

I have **soar**.

Who has the synonym
for **look**?

I Have, Who Has?: Language Arts • 1–2 © 2007 Creative Teaching Press

Synonyms–Verbs

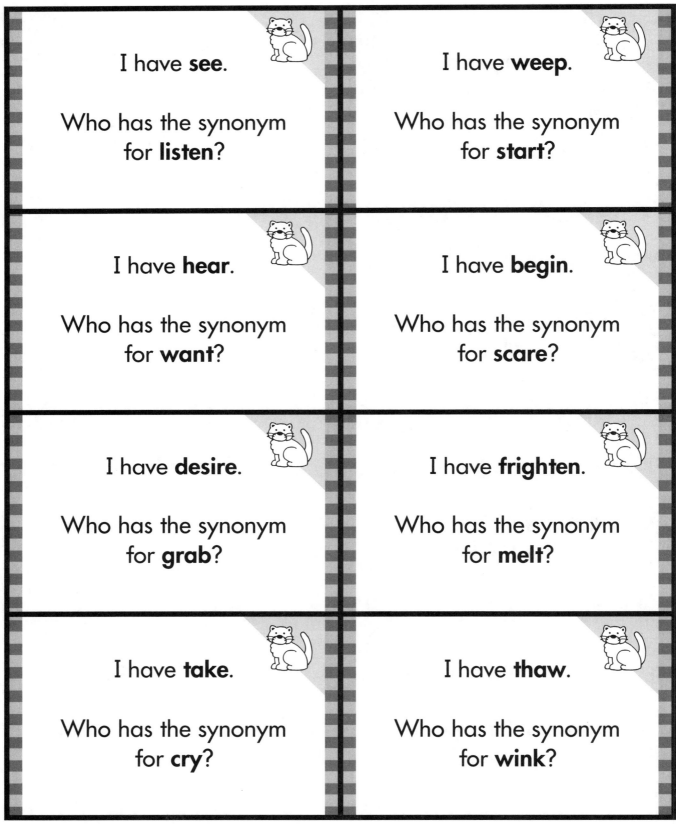

I have **see**.

Who has the synonym for **listen**?

I have **weep**.

Who has the synonym for **start**?

I have **hear**.

Who has the synonym for **want**?

I have **begin**.

Who has the synonym for **scare**?

I have **desire**.

Who has the synonym for **grab**?

I have **frighten**.

Who has the synonym for **melt**?

I have **take**.

Who has the synonym for **cry**?

I have **thaw**.

Who has the synonym for **wink**?

I Have, Who Has?: Language Arts • 1–2 © 2007 Creative Teaching Press

Synonyms–Verbs

I have **blink**.

Who has the synonym for **brag**?

I have **hurry**.

Who has the synonym for **create**?

I have **boast**.

Who has the synonym for **donate**?

I have **invent**.

Who has the synonym for **rest**?

I have **give**.

Who has the synonym for **giggle**?

I have **relax**.

Who has the synonym for **shock**?

I have **laugh**.

Who has the synonym for **rush**?

I have **surprise**.

Who has the **first card**?

I Have, Who Has?: Language Arts • 1–2 © 2007 Creative Teaching Press

Name _____ Date _____

Synonyms—Verbs

I Follow the path by coloring the verbs as your classmates name them.

*Start	fetch	crack	close
question	finish	cure	jump
scream	dwell	go	It's
take	desire	own	open
weep	hear	the	excuse
begin	see	soar	hold
frighten	penguin	give	laugh
thaw	blink	boast	hurry
*Finish	surprise	relax	invent

 II **Fun Fact: What is a bird that swims but cannot fly?**

Write the words left over in order on the lines below to answer the Fun Fact question.

Solution: _____ _____ _____.

III Write synonyms for the words that start with the letter "f."

1. _____ is a synonym for _____

2. _____ is a synonym for _____

3. _____ is a synonym for _____

Synonyms—Adjectives

I have the **first card**.

Who has the synonym
for **easy**?

I have **below**.

Who has the synonym
for **fat**?

I have **simple**.

Who has the synonym
for **brave**?

I have **plump**.

Who has the synonym
for **glad**?

I have **daring**.

Who has the synonym
for **scary**?

I have **happy**.

Who has the synonym
for **difficult**?

I have **frightful**.

Who has the synonym
for **under**?

I have **hard**.

Who has the synonym
for **kind**?

Synonyms–Adjectives

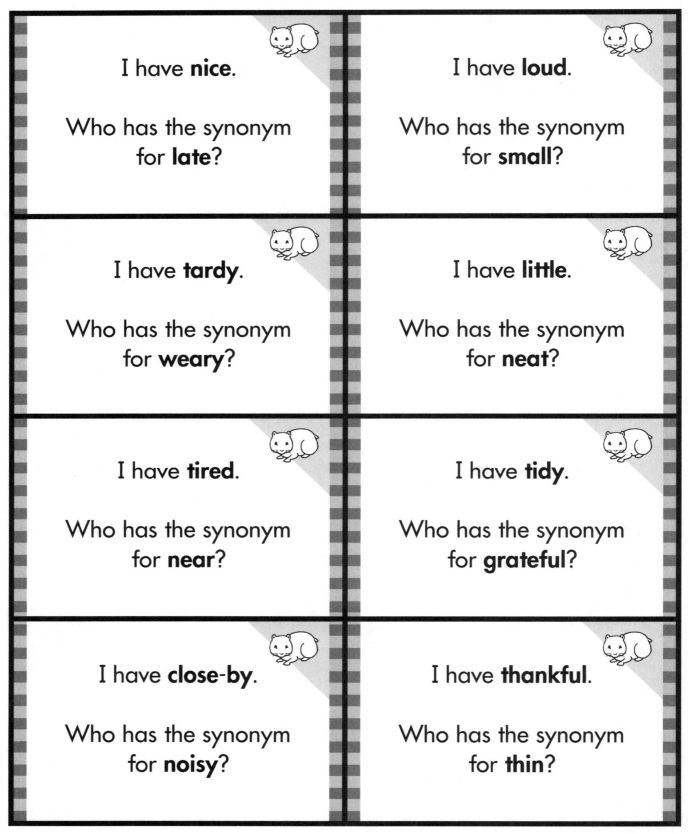

I have **nice**.

Who has the synonym
for **late**?

I have **loud**.

Who has the synonym
for **small**?

I have **tardy**.

Who has the synonym
for **weary**?

I have **little**.

Who has the synonym
for **neat**?

I have **tired**.

Who has the synonym
for **near**?

I have **tidy**.

Who has the synonym
for **grateful**?

I have **close-by**.

Who has the synonym
for **noisy**?

I have **thankful**.

Who has the synonym
for **thin**?

I Have, Who Has?: Language Arts • 1–2 © 2007 Creative Teaching Press

Synonyms–Adjectives

I have **slim**.

Who has the synonym for **unique**?

I have **chilly**.

Who has the synonym for **dirty**?

I have **special**.

Who has the synonym for **tasty**?

I have **filthy**.

Who has the synonym for **strong**?

I have **delicious**.

Who has the synonym for **grumpy**?

I have **powerful**.

Who has the synonym for **quick**?

I have **cranky**.

Who has the synonym for **cold**?

I have **fast**.

Who has the synonym for **correct**?

I Have, Who Has?: Language Arts • 1–2 © 2007 Creative Teaching Press

Synonyms—Adjectives

I have **right**.

Who has the synonym for **bent**?

I have **new**.

Who has the synonym for **rich**?

I have **twisted**.

Who has the synonym for **false**?

I have **wealthy**.

Who has the synonym for **fit**?

I have **fake**.

Who has the synonym for **quiet**?

I have **healthy**.

Who has the synonym for **sad**?

I have **silent**.

Who has the synonym for **fresh**?

I have **unhappy**.

Who has the **first card**?

I Have, Who Has?: Language Arts • 1–2 © 2007 Creative Teaching Press

Synonyms–Adjectives

I Follow the path by coloring the adjectives as your classmates name them.

*Start	simple	daring	frightful	below	plump
cranky	chilly	filthy	powerful	fast	happy
delicious				right	hard
special	healthy	unhappy	*Finish	twisted	nice
slim	wealthy	new	silent	fake	tardy
thankful	tidy	little	loud	close-by	tired
A	**B**	**C**	**D**	**E**	**F**

II In the blank box above, write a synonym for your favorite word.

III Write synonyms for three of the words in Column B.

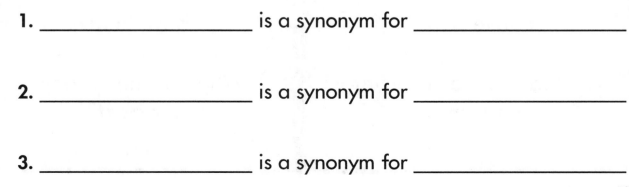

1. _____ is a synonym for _____

2. _____ is a synonym for _____

3. _____ is a synonym for _____

I Have, Who Has? Language Arts • 1–2 © 2007 Creative Teaching Press

Synonyms—Mixed Practice

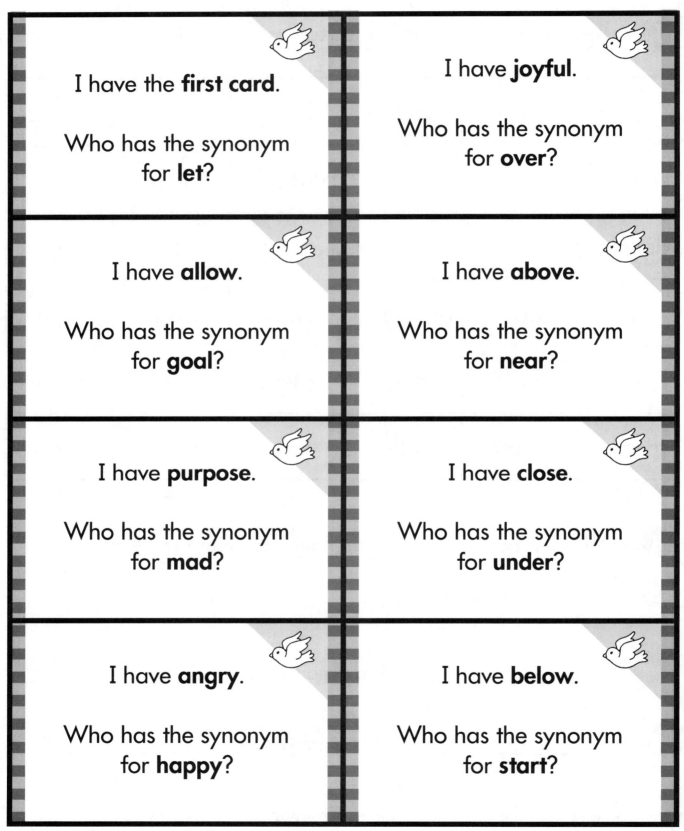

I have the **first card**.

Who has the synonym for **let**?

I have **joyful**.

Who has the synonym for **over**?

I have **allow**.

Who has the synonym for **goal**?

I have **above**.

Who has the synonym for **near**?

I have **purpose**.

Who has the synonym for **mad**?

I have **close**.

Who has the synonym for **under**?

I have **angry**.

Who has the synonym for **happy**?

I have **below**.

Who has the synonym for **start**?

I Have, Who Has?: Language Arts • 1–2 © 2007 Creative Teaching Press

Synonyms–Mixed Practice

I have **begin**.

Who has the synonym
for **go**?

I have **waste**.

Who has the synonym
for **job**?

I have **leave**.

Who has the synonym
for **donate**?

I have **task**.

Who has the synonym
for **small**?

I have **give**.

Who has the synonym
for **help**?

I have **little**.

Who has the synonym
for **glance**?

I have **aid**.

Who has the synonym
for **trash**?

I have **look**.

Who has the synonym
for **make**?

Synonyms—Mixed Practice

I have **create**.

Who has the synonym for **chat**?

I have **unkind**.

Who has the synonym for **tidy**?

I have **talk**.

Who has the synonym for **loud**?

I have **clean**.

Who has the synonym for **thin**?

I have **noisy**.

Who has the synonym for **big**?

I have **skinny**.

Who has the synonym for **dinner**?

I have **large**.

Who has the synonym for **mean**?

I have **supper**.

Who has the synonym for **easy**?

I Have, Who Has?: Language Arts • 1–2 © 2007 Creative Teaching Press

Synonyms–Mixed Practice

I have **simple**.

Who has the synonym for **real**?

I have **aged**.

Who has the synonym for **tired**?

I have **true**.

Who has the synonym for **equal**?

I have **sleepy**.

Who has the synonym for **crush**?

I have **same**.

Who has the synonym for **wise**?

I have **smash**.

Who has the synonym for **collect**?

I have **smart**.

Who has the synonym for **old**?

I have **gather**.

Who has the **first card**?

Name _____ Date _____

Synonyms–Mixed Practice

I Follow the path by coloring the words as your classmates name them.

*Start	allow	joyful	above
It	purpose	angry	close
same	true	takes	below
smart	simple	leave	begin
aged	supper	give	aid
sleepy	skinny	task	waste
smash	clean	little	look
gather	unkind	large	create
*Finish	dozen	noisy	talk

II **Fun Fact: How many honeybees does it take to make a teaspoon of honey?**

Write the words left over on the lines below to answer the Fun Fact question.

Solution: _____ _____ a _____.

III Write synonyms for three words in the table that have two syllables.

1. _____ is a synonym for _____

2. _____ is a synonym for _____

3. _____ is a synonym for _____

I Have, Who Has?: Language Arts • 1–2 © 2007 Creative Teaching Press

Antonyms—Nouns

I have the **first card**.

Who has the antonym
for **sunlight**?

I have **student**.

Who has the antonym
for **happiness**?

I have **moonlight**.

Who has the antonym
for **fact**?

I have **sadness**.

Who has the antonym
for **question**?

I have **fiction**.

Who has the antonym
for **black**?

I have **answer**.

Who has the antonym
for **beginning**?

I have **white**.

Who has the antonym
for **teacher**?

I have **ending**.

Who has the antonym
for **danger**?

Antonym-Nouns

I have **safety**.

Who has the antonym for **girl**?

I have **entrance**.

Who has the antonym for **whole**?

I have **boy**.

Who has the antonym for **sunrise**?

I have **part**.

Who has the antonym for **brother**?

I have **sunset**.

Who has the antonym for **friend**?

I have **sister**.

Who has the antonym for **laugh**?

I have **enemy**.

Who has the antonym for **exit**?

I have **cry**.

Who has the antonym for **war**?

Antonyms–Nouns

I have **peace**.

Who has the antonym
for **antonym**?

I have **punishment**.

Who has the antonym
for **leader**?

I have **synonym**.

Who has the antonym
for **gain**?

I have **follower**.

Who has the antonym
for **woman**?

I have **loss**.

Who has the antonym
for **success**?

I have **man**.

Who has the antonym
for **work**?

I have **failure**.

Who has the antonym
for **reward**?

I have **play**.

Who has the antonym
for **night**?

Antonym–Nouns

I have **day**.

Who has the antonym for **dry**?

I have **king**.

Who has the antonym for **parent**?

I have **wet**.

Who has the antonym for **doctor**?

I have **child**.

Who has the antonym for **summer**?

I have **patient**.

Who has the antonym for **ceiling**?

I have **winter**.

Who has the antonym for **country**?

I have **floor**.

Who has the antonym for **queen**?

I have **city**.

Who has the **first card**?

I Have, Who Has?: Language Arts • 1–2 © 2007 Creative Teaching Press

Name _____ Date _____

Antonyms—Nouns

I Follow the path by coloring the noun as your classmates name them.

*Start	white	student	ending	safety	boy
moonlight	fiction	sadness	answer	enemy	sunset
patient	wet	day	play	entrance	part
floor	king	child	man	cry	sister
*Finish	city	winter	follower	peace	synonym
			punishment	failure	loss
A	**B**	**C**	**D**	**E**	**F**

II Write an antonym for your favorite noun in the blank box above.

III Write antonyms for three nouns in Column F.

1. _____ is an antonym for _____

2. _____ is an antonym for _____

3. _____ is an antonym for _____

Antonyms–Verbs

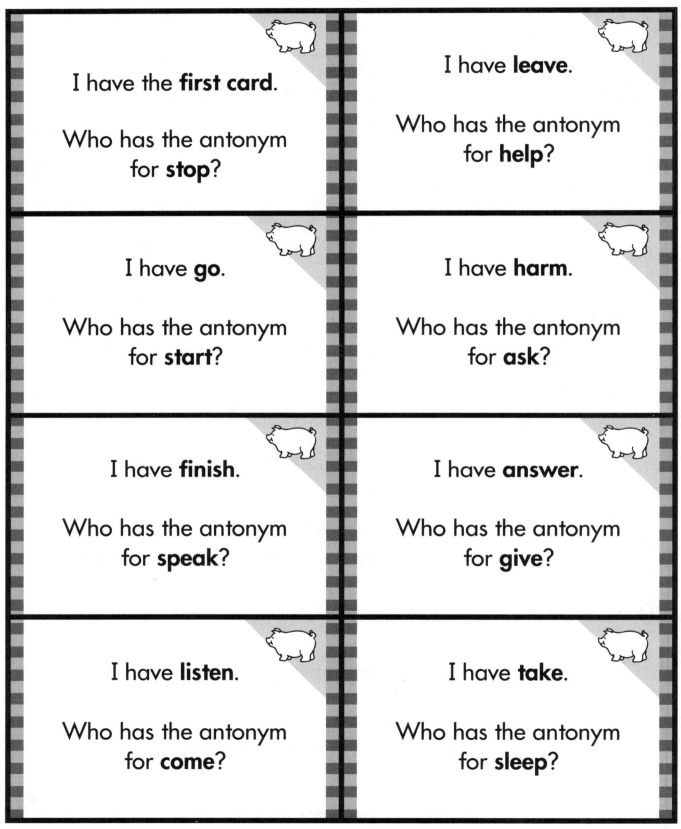

I have the **first card**.

Who has the antonym for **stop**?

I have **leave**.

Who has the antonym for **help**?

I have **go**.

Who has the antonym for **start**?

I have **harm**.

Who has the antonym for **ask**?

I have **finish**.

Who has the antonym for **speak**?

I have **answer**.

Who has the antonym for **give**?

I have **listen**.

Who has the antonym for **come**?

I have **take**.

Who has the antonym for **sleep**?

I Have, Who Has?: Language Arts • 1–2 © 2007 Creative Teaching Press

Antonyms—Verbs

I have **wake**.

Who has the antonym
for **agree**?

I have **fix**.

Who has the antonym
for **create**?

I have **disagree**.

Who has the antonym
for **like**?

I have **destroy**.

Who has the antonym
for **shrink**?

I have **dislike**.

Who has the antonym
for **buy**?

I have **stretch**.

Who has the antonym
for **win**?

I have **sell**.

Who has the antonym
for **break**?

I have **lose**.

Who has the antonym
for **soften**?

Antonyms–Verbs

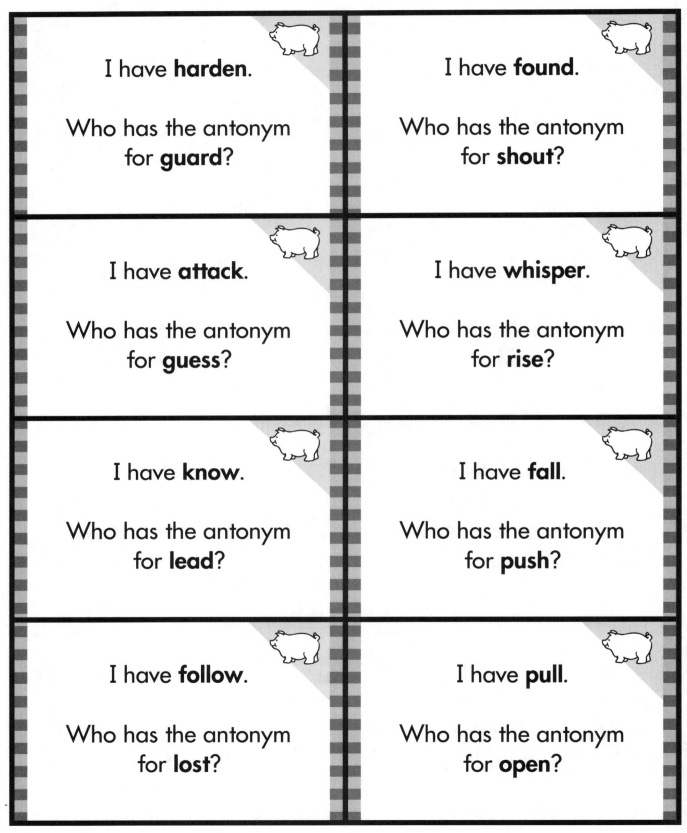

I have **harden**.

Who has the antonym for **guard**?

I have **found**.

Who has the antonym for **shout**?

I have **attack**.

Who has the antonym for **guess**?

I have **whisper**.

Who has the antonym for **rise**?

I have **know**.

Who has the antonym for **lead**?

I have **fall**.

Who has the antonym for **push**?

I have **follow**.

Who has the antonym for **lost**?

I have **pull**.

Who has the antonym for **open**?

Antonyms—Verbs

I have **close**.

Who has the antonym for **live**?

I have **subtract**.

Who has the antonym for **sit**?

I have **die**.

Who has the antonym for **freeze**?

I have **stand**.

Who has the antonym for **smile**?

I have **thaw**.

Who has the antonym for **combine**?

I have **frown**.

Who has the antonym for **sink**?

I have **separate**.

Who has the antonym for **add**?

I have **float**.

Who has the **first card**?

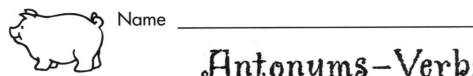

Name _____ Date _____

Antonyms—Verbs

I Follow the path by coloring the verbs as your classmates name them.

*Start	lose	harden	Only
go	stretch	attack	know
finish	destroy	fix	follow
listen	leave	sell	found
answer	harm	dislike	whisper
take	wake	disagree	fall
*Finish	float	close	pull
males	frown	die	thaw
gobble	stand	subtract	separate

II **Fun Fact: What can male turkeys do that female turkeys cannot?**

Write the words left over in order on the lines below to answer the Fun Fact question. Circle the verb in the solution below.

Solution: _____ **the** _____ _____ .

III Write an antonym for two verbs that have one syllable.

1. _____ is an antonym for _____

2. _____ is an antonym for _____

I Have, Who Has?: Language Arts • 1–2 © 2007 Creative Teaching Press

Antonyms–Adjectives

I have the **first card**.

Who has the antonym
for **cold**?

I have **bad**.

Who has the antonym
for **nice**?

I have **hot**.

Who has the antonym
for **hard**?

I have **mean**.

Who has the antonym
for **pretty**?

I have **soft**.

Who has the antonym
for **easy**?

I have **ugly**.

Who has the antonym
for **short**?

I have **difficult**.

Who has the antonym
for **good**?

I have **tall**.

Who has the antonym
for **above**?

Antonyms–Adjectives

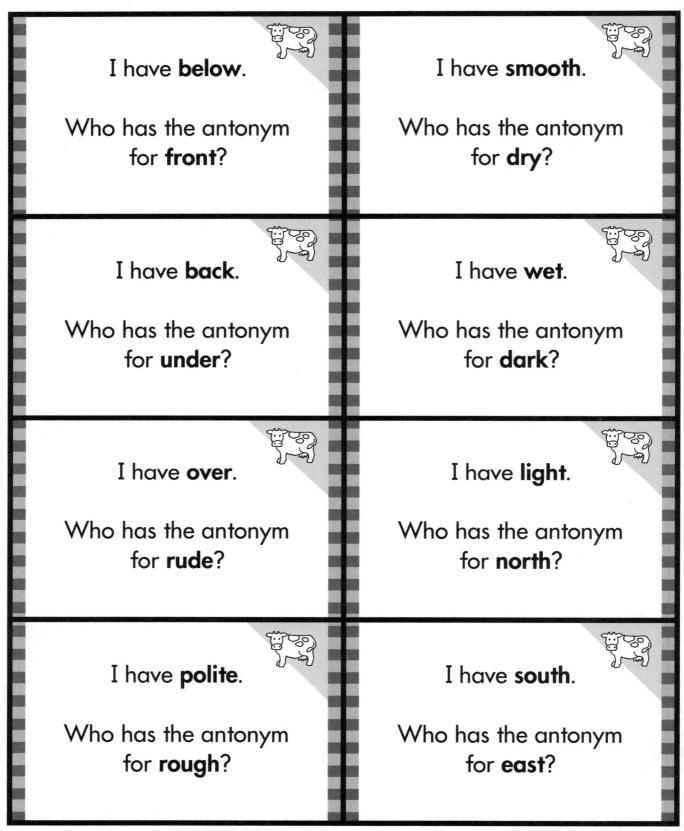

I have **below**.

Who has the antonym for **front**?

I have **smooth**.

Who has the antonym for **dry**?

I have **back**.

Who has the antonym for **under**?

I have **wet**.

Who has the antonym for **dark**?

I have **over**.

Who has the antonym for **rude**?

I have **light**.

Who has the antonym for **north**?

I have **polite**.

Who has the antonym for **rough**?

I have **south**.

Who has the antonym for **east**?

I Have, Who Has?: Language Arts • 1–2 © 2007 Creative Teaching Press

Antonyms–Adjectives

I have **west**.

Who has the antonym for **new**?

I have **before**.

Who has the antonym for **awake**?

I have **old**.

Who has the antonym for **empty**?

I have **asleep**.

Who has the antonym for **deep**?

I have **full**.

Who has the antonym for **fair**?

I have **shallow**.

Who has the antonym for **sharp**?

I have **unfair**.

Who has the antonym for **after**?

I have **dull**.

Who has the antonym for **even**?

Antonyms–Adjectives

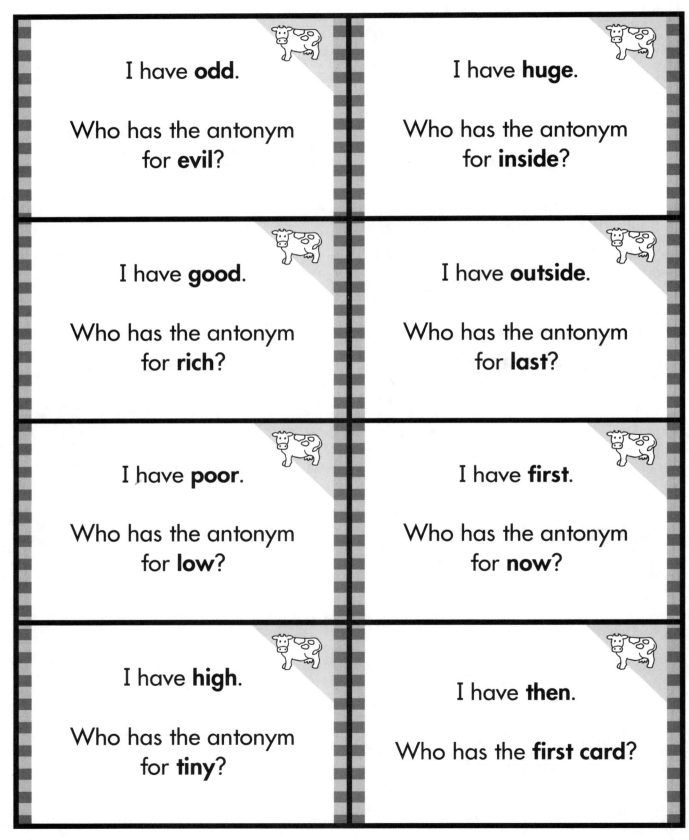

I have **odd**.

Who has the antonym for **evil**?

I have **huge**.

Who has the antonym for **inside**?

I have **good**.

Who has the antonym for **rich**?

I have **outside**.

Who has the antonym for **last**?

I have **poor**.

Who has the antonym for **low**?

I have **first**.

Who has the antonym for **now**?

I have **high**.

Who has the antonym for **tiny**?

I have **then**.

Who has the **first card**?

Name _____ Date _____

Antonyms—Adjectives

I Follow the path by coloring the adjectives as your classmates name them.

*Start	hot	soft	difficult	ugly	tall
old	west	south	bad	mean	below
full	unfair	light	polite	over	back
asleep	before	wet	smooth	outside	first
shallow	good	poor	high	huge	then
dull	odd				*Finish
A	**B**	**C**	**D**	**E**	**F**

II Write an antonym for your favorite adjective in the blank box above.

III For four adjectives in Column D, write an antonym on the line below.

1. _____ is an antonym for _____

2. _____ is an antonym for _____

3. _____ is an antonym for _____

4. _____ is an antonym for _____

I Have, Who Has? Language Arts • 1–2 © 2007 Creative Teaching Press

Antonyms–Mixed Practice

I have the **first card**.

Who has the antonym
for **alone**?

I have **repair**.

Who has the antonym
for **clean**?

I have **together**.

Who has the antonym
for **bitter**?

I have **dirty**.

Who has the antonym
for **open**?

I have **sweet**.

Who has the antonym
for **shy**?

I have **close**.

Who has the antonym
for **crooked**?

I have **outgoing**.

Who has the antonym
for **break**?

I have **straight**.

Who has the antonym
for **dawn**?

I Have, Who Has?: Language Arts • 1–2 © 2007 Creative Teaching Press

Antonyms–Mixed Practice

I have **dusk**.

Who has the antonym for **dim**?

I have **harsh**.

Who has the antonym for **heavy**?

I have **bright**.

Who has the antonym for **blame**?

I have **light**.

Who has the antonym for **hill**?

I have **praise**.

Who has the antonym for **selfish**?

I have **valley**.

Who has the antonym for **hire**?

I have **giving**.

Who has the antonym for **gentle**?

I have **fire**.

Who has the antonym for **him**?

I Have, Who Has?: Language Arts • 1–2 © 2007 Creative Teaching Press

Antonyms—Mixed Practice

I have **her**.

Who has the antonym
for **mine**?

I have **out**.

Who has the antonym
for **free**?

I have **yours**.

Who has the antonym
for **she**?

I have **costly**.

Who has the antonym
for **left**?

I have **he**.

Who has the antonym
for **jolly**?

I have **right**.

Who has the antonym
for **fact**?

I have **serious**.

Who has the antonym
for **in**?

I have **fiction**.

Who has the antonym
for **wide**?

I Have, Who Has?: Language Arts • 1–2 © 2007 Creative Teaching Press

Antonyms-Mixed Practice

I have **narrow**.

Who has the antonym
for **less**?

I have **least**.

Who has the antonym
for **you**?

I have **more**.

Who has the antonym
for **many**?

I have **me**.

Who has the antonym
for **save**?

I have **few**.

Who has the antonym
for **melt**?

I have **spend**.

Who has the antonym
for **near**?

I have **freeze**.

Who has the antonym
for **most**?

I have **far**.

Who has the **first card**?

Antonyms—Mixed Practice

I Follow the path by coloring the words as your classmates name them.

*Start	outgoing	repair	dirty
together	sweet	sleep	close
out	serious	dusk	straight
costly	he	bright	praise
right	yours	eye	giving
fiction	her	fire	harsh
narrow	more	valley	light
freeze	few	far	*Finish
least	me	spend	open

II **Fun Fact: What is unusual about how dolphins sleep?**

Write the words left over on the lines below to answer the Fun Fact question.

Solution: They _____ with one _____ _____.

III What is an antonym for the verb in the solution? _____

IV Write an antonym for three of the words above that have two syllables.

1. _____ is an antonym for _____

2. _____ is an antonym for _____

3. _____ is an antonym for _____

I Have, Who Has?: Language Arts • 1–2 © 2007 Creative Teaching Press

Basic Analogies

I have the **first card**.

Who has the word to finish this analogy?
back is to **rear**
as
over is to _____

I have **question**.

Who has the word to finish this analogy?
awake is to **asleep**
as
ugly is to _____

I have **above**.

Who has the word to finish this analogy?
up is to **down**
as
in is to _____

I have **pretty**.

Who has the word to finish this analogy?
open is to **shut**
as
moon is to _____

I have **out**.

Who has the word to finish this analogy?
good is to **bad**
as
soft is to _____

I have **sun**.

Who has the word to finish this analogy?
even is to **odd**
as
top is to _____

I have **hard**.

Who has the word to finish this analogy?
look is to **see**
as
ask is to _____

I have **bottom**.

Who has the word to finish this analogy?
join is to **add**
as
separate is to _____

Basic Analogies

I have **subtract**.

Who has the word to finish this analogy?
fix is to **mend**
as
yell is to _____

I have **chair**.

Who has the word to finish this analogy?
ill is to **sick**
as
thin is to _____

I have **shout**.

Who has the word to finish this analogy?
enter is to **exit**
as
black is to _____

I have **slim**.

Who has the word to finish this analogy?
clean is to **dirty**
as
beginning is to _____

I have **white**.

Who has the word to finish this analogy?
low is to **high**
as
empty is to _____

I have **end**.

Who has the word to finish this analogy?
start is to **begin**
as
end is to _____

I have **full**.

Who has the word to finish this analogy?
job is to **task**
as
seat is to _____

I have **finish**.

Who has the word to finish this analogy?
cause is to **effect**
as
day is to _____

I Have, Who Has?: Language Arts • 1–2 © 2007 Creative Teaching Press

Basic Analogies

I have **night**.

Who has the word to finish this analogy?
small is to **large**
as
light is to _____

I have **clear**.

Who has the word to finish this analogy?
duo is to **two**
as
trio is to _____

I have **heavy**.

Who has the word to finish this analogy?
go is to **leave**
as
happy is to _____

I have **three**.

Who has the word to finish this analogy?
east is to **west**
as
north is to _____

I have **glad**.

Who has the word to finish this analogy?
funny is to **scary**
as
dark is to _____

I have **south**.

Who has the word to finish this analogy?
strong is to **powerful**
as
huge is to _____

I have **bright**.

Who has the word to finish this analogy?
near is to **far**
as
blurry is to _____

I have **giant**.

Who has the word to finish this analogy?
laugh is to **cry**
as
smile is to _____

Basic Analogies

I have **frown**.

Who has the word to finish this analogy?
rough is to **smooth**
as
wet is to _____

I have **old**.

Who has the word to finish this analogy?
baby is to **infant**
as
student is to _____

I have **dry**.

Who has the word to finish this analogy?
he is to **she**
as
man is to _____

I have **learner**.

Who has the word to finish this analogy?
make is to **create**
as
hold is to _____

I have **woman**.

Who has the word to finish this analogy?
help is to **aid**
as
listen is to _____

I have **carry**.

Who has the word to finish this analogy?
wide is to **narrow**
as
yes is to _____

I have **hear**.

Who has the word to finish this analogy?
more is to **less**
as
new is to _____

I have **no**.

Who has the **first card**?

I Have, Who Has?: Language Arts • 1–2 © 2007 Creative Teaching Press

Name _____ Date _____

Basic Analogies

I Follow the path by coloring the words as your classmates name them.

*Start	full	chair	slim	end	finish
above	white	bright	glad	heavy	night
out	shout	clear	three	south	giant
hard	subtract	hear	woman	dry	frown
question	bottom	old	learner	carry	no
pretty	sun				*Finish

II Write an analogy of your own in the blank box above.

III Finish each analogy. Circle what type of analogy it is.

1. sunny is to **cloudy** as **warm** is to _____   synonym   antonym

2. sad is to **funny** as **empty** is to _____   synonym   antonym

3. large is to **big** as **tiny** is to _____   synonym   antonym

4. end is to **finish** as **start** is to _____   synonym   antonym

Advanced Analogies

I have the **first card**.

Who has the word to finish this analogy?
finger is to **hand**
as
toe is to _____

I have **kitchen**.

Who has the word to finish this analogy?
hand is to **clock**
as
wheel is to _____

I have **foot**.

Who has the word to finish this analogy?
sky is to **blue**
as
grass is to _____

I have **car**.

Who has the word to finish this analogy?
honey is to **sticky**
as
ice is to _____

I have **green**.

Who has the word to finish this analogy?
sun is to **heat**
as
brain is to _____

I have **cold**.

Who has the word to finish this analogy?
bell is to **rings**
as
dog is to _____

I have **think**.

Who has the word to finish this analogy?
tub is to **bathroom**
as
oven is to _____

I have **barks**.

Who has the word to finish this analogy?
crayon is to **crayon box**
as
book is to _____

Advanced Analogies

I have **bookcase**.

Who has the word to finish this analogy?
screen is to **computer**
as
page is to _____

I have **hive**.

Who has the word to finish this analogy?
timer is to **buzzes**
as
phone is to _____

I have **book**.

Who has the word to finish this analogy?
sandpaper is to **rough**
as
rabbit is to _____

I have **rings**.

Who has the word to finish this analogy?
fish is to **school**
as
deer is to _____

I have **fluffy**.

Who has the word to finish this analogy?
foot is to **kick**
as
eye is to _____

I have **herd**.

Who has the word to finish this analogy?
concert is to **loud**
as
library is to _____

I have **see**.

Who has the word to finish this analogy?
bear is to **den**
as
bee is to _____

I have **quiet**.

Who has the word to finish this analogy?
horse is to **gallops**
as
turtle is to _____

I Have, Who Has? Language Arts • 1–2 © 2007 Creative Teaching Press

Advanced Analogies

I have **crawls.**

Who has the word to finish this analogy?
bird is to **nest**
as
whale is to _____

I have **sails.**

Who has the word to finish this analogy?
cow is to **farm**
as
tiger is to _____

I have **ocean.**

Who has the word to finish this analogy?
button is to **shirt**
as
lace is to _____

I have **jungle.**

Who has the word to finish this analogy?
eraser is to **pencil**
as
tooth is to _____

I have **shoe.**

Who has the word to finish this analogy?
rain is to **wet**
as
sandpaper is to _____

I have **mouth.**

Who has the word to finish this analogy?
night is to **dark**
as
water is to _____

I have **rough.**

Who has the word to finish this analogy?
plane is to **flies**
as
ship is to _____

I have **wet.**

Who has the word to finish this analogy?
ice is to **melts**
as
trash is to _____

I Have, Who Has?: Language Arts • 1–2 © 2007 Creative Teaching Press

Advanced Analogies

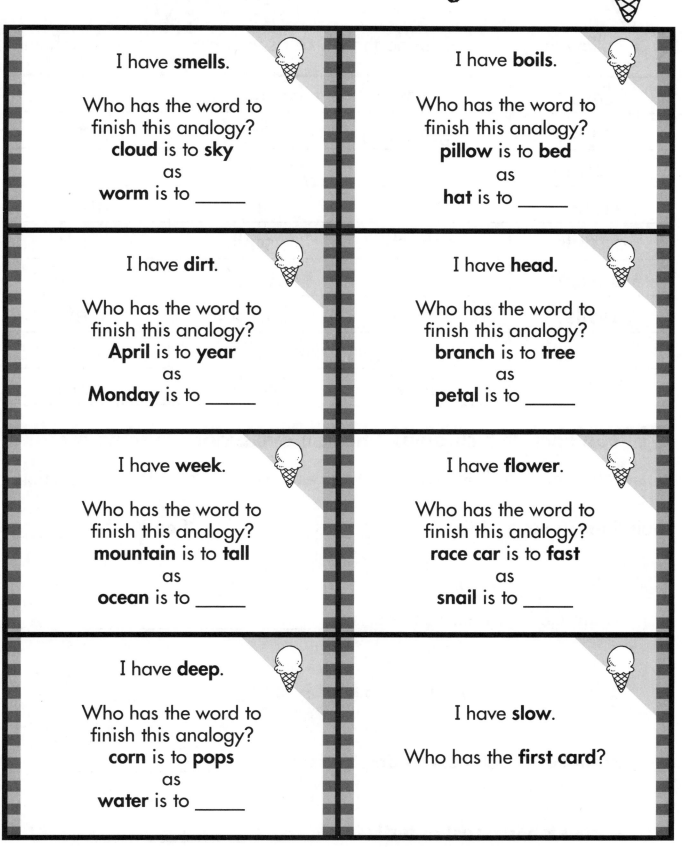

I have **smells**.

Who has the word to finish this analogy?
cloud is to **sky**
as
worm is to _____

I have **boils**.

Who has the word to finish this analogy?
pillow is to **bed**
as
hat is to _____

I have **dirt**.

Who has the word to finish this analogy?
April is to **year**
as
Monday is to _____

I have **head**.

Who has the word to finish this analogy?
branch is to **tree**
as
petal is to _____

I have **week**.

Who has the word to finish this analogy?
mountain is to **tall**
as
ocean is to _____

I have **flower**.

Who has the word to finish this analogy?
race car is to **fast**
as
snail is to _____

I have **deep**.

Who has the word to finish this analogy?
corn is to **pops**
as
water is to _____

I have **slow**.

Who has the **first card**?

Advanced Analogies

I Follow the path by coloring the words as your classmates name them.

*Start	foot	bookcase	book
think	green	barks	fluffy
kitchen	car	cold	see
quiet	herd	rings	hive
crawls	ostrich	sails	jungle
ocean	shoe	rough	mouth
boils	deep	bigger	wet
head	week	dirt	smells
flower	slow	*Finish	brain

II **Fun Fact: Which animal has an eye bigger than its brain?**

Write the words left over on the lines to answer the Fun Fact question.

Solution: The eye of the _____ is _____ than its _____.

III Finish each analogy.

1. **mouse** is to **hole** as **letter** is to _____

2. **inventor** is to **creates** as **doctor** is to _____

3. **snake** is to **slithers** as **dolphin** is to _____

4. **cheetah** is to **fast** as **turtle** is to _____

I Have, Who Has?: Language Arts • 1–2 © 2007 Creative Teaching Press

Identify the Contraction

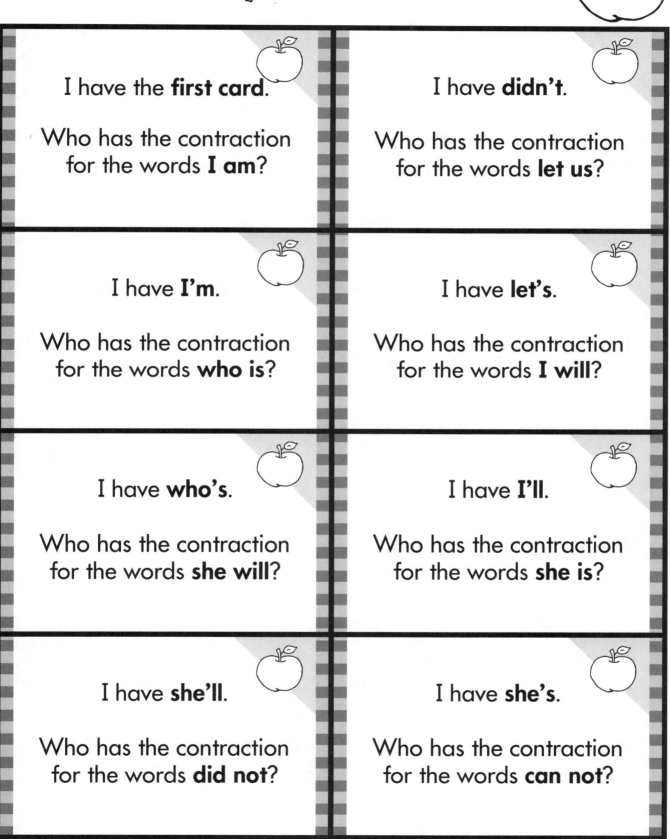

I have the **first card**.

Who has the contraction
for the words **I am**?

I have **didn't**.

Who has the contraction
for the words **let us**?

I have **I'm**.

Who has the contraction
for the words **who is**?

I have **let's**.

Who has the contraction
for the words **I will**?

I have **who's**.

Who has the contraction
for the words **she will**?

I have **I'll**.

Who has the contraction
for the words **she is**?

I have **she'll**.

Who has the contraction
for the words **did not**?

I have **she's**.

Who has the contraction
for the words **can not**?

Identify the Contraction

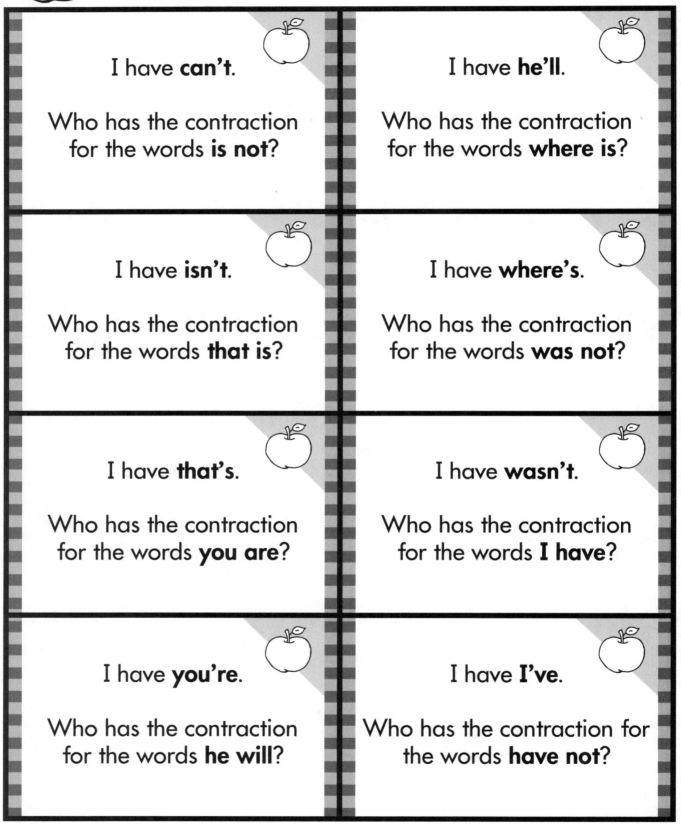

I have **can't**.

Who has the contraction for the words **is not**?

I have **he'll**.

Who has the contraction for the words **where is**?

I have **isn't**.

Who has the contraction for the words **that is**?

I have **where's**.

Who has the contraction for the words **was not**?

I have **that's**.

Who has the contraction for the words **you are**?

I have **wasn't**.

Who has the contraction for the words **I have**?

I have **you're**.

Who has the contraction for the words **he will**?

I have **I've**.

Who has the contraction for the words **have not**?

Identify the Contraction

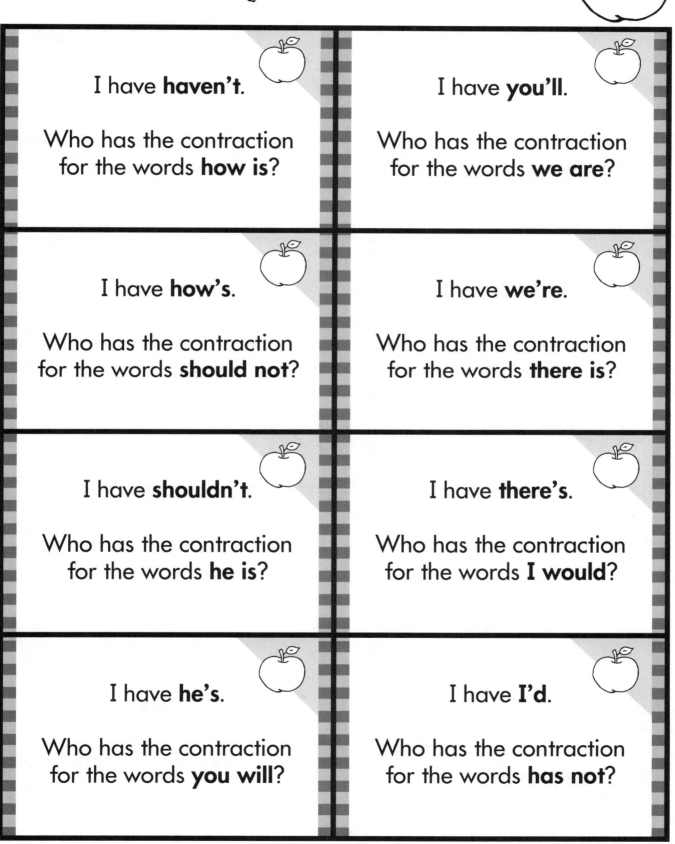

I have **haven't**.

Who has the contraction for the words **how is**?

I have **you'll**.

Who has the contraction for the words **we are**?

I have **how's**.

Who has the contraction for the words **should not**?

I have **we're**.

Who has the contraction for the words **there is**?

I have **shouldn't**.

Who has the contraction for the words **he is**?

I have **there's**.

Who has the contraction for the words **I would**?

I have **he's**.

Who has the contraction for the words **you will**?

I have **I'd**.

Who has the contraction for the words **has not**?

I Have, Who Has? Language Arts • 1–2 © 2007 Creative Teaching Press

Identify the Contraction

I have **hasn't**.

Who has the contraction for the words **they will**?

I have **don't**.

Who has the contraction for the words **what is**?

I have **they'll**.

Who has the contraction for the words **we have**?

I have **what's**.

Who has the contraction for the words **will not**?

I have **we've**.

Who has the contraction for the words **it is**?

I have **won't**.

Who has the contraction for the words **they are**?

I have **it's**.

Who has the contraction for the words **do not**?

I have **they're**.

Who has the **first card**?

Name _____ Date _____

Identify the Contraction

I Follow the path by coloring the contractions as your classmates name them.

*Start	I'm	he'll	where's	wasn't	I've
she'll	who's	you're	that's	isn't	haven't
didn't	let's	I'll	she's	can't	how's
it's	we've	they'll	hasn't	I'd	shouldn't
don't	what's	won't	they're	there's	he's
			*Finish	we're	you'll

A   **B**   **C**   **D**   **E**   **F**

II Write a contraction using the word **we** in the blank box above.

III Write the words that make up three of the contractions in Column F.

1. _____ is made up of the words _____ and _____

2. _____ is made up of the words _____ and _____

3. _____ is made up of the words _____ and _____

I Have, Who Has? Language Arts • 1–2 © 2007 Creative Teaching Press

Identify the Words for Each Contraction

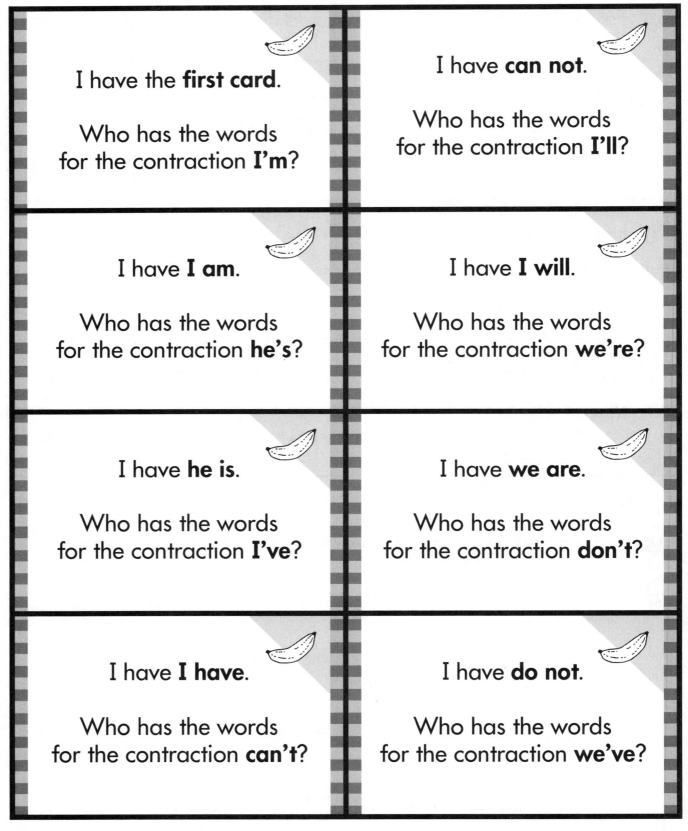

I have the **first card**.

Who has the words
for the contraction **I'm**?

I have **can not**.

Who has the words
for the contraction **I'll**?

I have **I am**.

Who has the words
for the contraction **he's**?

I have **I will**.

Who has the words
for the contraction **we're**?

I have **he is**.

Who has the words
for the contraction **I've**?

I have **we are**.

Who has the words
for the contraction **don't**?

I have **I have**.

Who has the words
for the contraction **can't**?

I have **do not**.

Who has the words
for the contraction **we've**?

I Have, Who Has?: Language Arts • 1–2 © 2007 Creative Teaching Press

Identify the Words for Each Contraction

I have **we have**.

Who has the words for the contraction **who's**?

I have **she is**.

Who has the words for the contraction **isn't**?

I have **who is**.

Who has the words for the contraction **let's**?

I have **is not**.

Who has the words for the contraction **she'll**?

I have **let us**.

Who has the words for the contraction **who'll**?

I have **she will**.

Who has the words for the contraction **you're**?

I have **who will**.

Who has the words for the contraction **she's**?

I have **you are**.

Who has the words for the contraction **hasn't**?

Identify the Words for Each Contraction

I have **has not**.

Who has the words for the contraction **aren't**?

I have **they are**.

Who has the words for the contraction **doesn't**?

I have **are not**.

Who has the words for the contraction **wasn't**?

I have **does not**.

Who has the words for the contraction **he'll**?

I have **was not**.

Who has the words for the contraction **here's**?

I have **he will**.

Who has the words for the contraction **it'll**?

I have **here is**.

Who has the words for the contraction **they're**?

I have **it will**.

Who has the words for the contraction **you've**?

I Have, Who Has?: Language Arts • 1–2 © 2007 Creative Teaching Press

Identify the Words for Each Contraction

I have **you have**.

Who has the words for the contraction **it's**?

I have **could not**.

Who has the words for the contraction **wouldn't**?

I have **it is**.

Who has the words for the contraction **that's**?

I have **would not**.

Who has the words for the contraction **shouldn't**?

I have **that is**.

Who has the words for the contraction **you'll**?

I have **should not**.

Who has the words for the contraction **we'll**?

I have **you will**.

Who has the words for the contraction **couldn't**?

I have **we will**.

Who has the **first card**?

I Have, Who Has?: Language Arts • 1–2 © 2007 Creative Teaching Press

Identify the Words for Each Contraction

I Follow the path by coloring the words as your classmates name them.

*Start	I am	he is	I have	can not
who will	let us	It	we are	I will
she is	who is	we have	do not	closes
is not	has not	are not	was not	here is
she will	you are	he will	does not	they are
it is	you have	it will	its	doors
that is	you will	could not	we will	*Finish
for	two	would not	should not	months
A	**B**	**C**	**D**	**E**

II **Fun Fact: Do you know what the zoo in Tokyo, Japan, does each year to give the animals a holiday from visitors?**

Write the words left over on the lines below to answer the Fun Fact question.

Solution:

_____ _____ _____ _____ _____ _____.

III Write the contraction that is made from two of the words in Column D.

1. _____ and _____ make the contraction _____

2. _____ and _____ make the contraction _____

I Have, Who Has?: Language Arts • 1–2 © 2007 Creative Teaching Press

Compound Words 1

I have the **first card**.

Who has the compound word used to say **your back hurts**?

I have **bedroom**.

Who has the compound word used to name **a fire at camp**?

I have **backache**.

Who has the compound word used to say **the place where a baseball game is played**?

I have **campfire**.

Who has the compound word used to name **the nail on your finger**?

I have **ballpark**.

Who has the compound word used to say **you are not wearing shoes**?

I have **fingernail**.

Who has the compound word used to name **the worm that lives under the ground**?

I have **barefoot**.

Who has the compound word used to say **where you sleep in your house**?

I have **earthworm**.

Who has the compound word used to name **the path to a home a car drives on**?

I Have, Who Has? Language Arts • 1–2 © 2007 Creative Teaching Press

Compound Words 1

I have **driveway**.

Who has the compound word used to name **a sport in which players try to tackle the player with the ball**.

I have **shoelace**.

Who has the compound word used to name **food that comes from the ocean**?

I have **football**.

Who has the compound word used to name **a "man" made out of snow**?

I have **seafood**.

Who has the compound word used to name **the paper that gives you the news**?

I have **snowman**.

Who has the compound word used to name **a shell found at the beach**?

I have **newspaper**.

Who has the compound word used to name **the light we get from the moon**?

I have **seashell**.

Who has the compound word used to name **the lace that ties your shoe**?

I have **moonlight**.

Who has the compound word used to name **a friend who is a girl**?

Compound Words 1

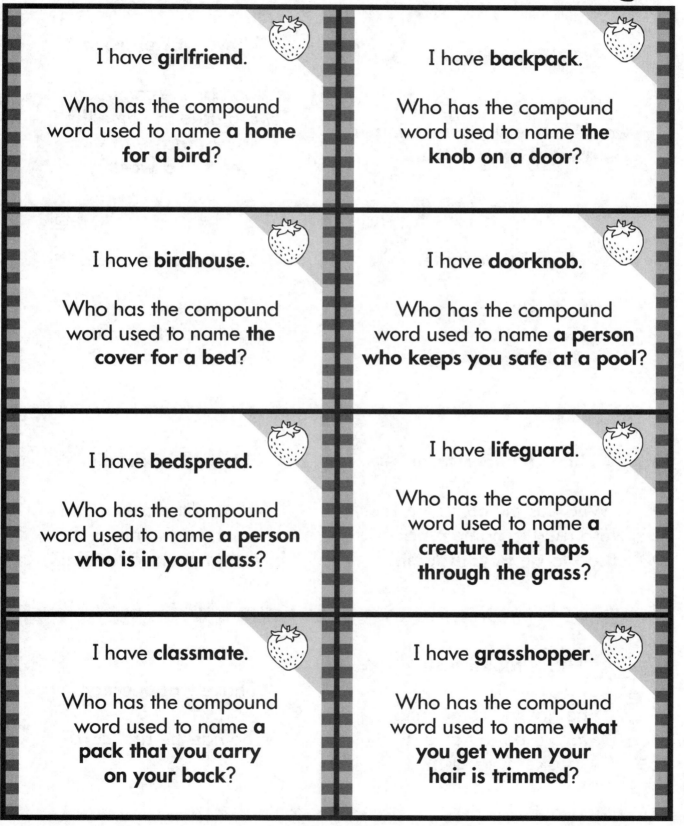

I have **girlfriend**.

Who has the compound word used to name **a home for a bird**?

I have **backpack**.

Who has the compound word used to name **the knob on a door**?

I have **birdhouse**.

Who has the compound word used to name **the cover for a bed**?

I have **doorknob**.

Who has the compound word used to name **a person who keeps you safe at a pool**?

I have **bedspread**.

Who has the compound word used to name **a person who is in your class**?

I have **lifeguard**.

Who has the compound word used to name **a creature that hops through the grass**?

I have **classmate**.

Who has the compound word used to name **a pack that you carry on your back**?

I have **grasshopper**.

Who has the compound word used to name **what you get when your hair is trimmed**?

Compound Words 1

I have **haircut**.

Who has the compound word used to say **something is created at your house**?

I have **wastebasket**.

Who has the compound word used to name **the days that are at the end of a week**?

I have **homemade**.

Who has the compound word used to name **a storm that has thunder**?

I have **weekend**.

Who has the compound word used to name **a chair on wheels**?

I have **thunderstorm**.

Who has the compound word used to name **a brush used to clean your teeth**?

I have **wheelchair**.

Who has the compound word used to name **a bird that pecks on wood**?

I have **toothbrush**.

Who has the compound word used to name **a basket for trash**?

I have **woodpecker**.

Who has the **first card**?

I Have, Who Has?: Language Arts • 1–2 © 2007 Creative Teaching Press

Name _____ Date _____

Compound Words 1

I Follow the path by coloring the compound words as your classmates name them.

*Start	backache	ballpark	barefoot	bedroom	campfire
moonlight	newspaper	seafood	shoelace	seashell	fingernail
girlfriend	birdhouse	bedspread	classmate	snowman	earthworm
grasshopper	lifeguard	doorknob	backpack	football	driveway
haircut	homemade	thunderstorm	toothbrush	wastebasket	weekend
			*Finish	woodpecker	wheelchair

A **B** **C** **D** **E** **F**

II Write a compound word of your own in the blank box above.

III Write the words that make up three of the compound words in Column E.

1. _____ is made up of the words _____ and _____

2. _____ is made up of the words _____ and _____

3. _____ is made up of the words _____ and _____

I Have, Who Has?: Language Arts • 1–2 © 2007 Creative Teaching Press

Compound Words 2

I have the **first card**.

Who has the compound word used to say **something is tight enough to keep air out**?

I have **earthquake**.

Who has the compound word used to name **the room where you take a bath**?

I have **airtight**.

Who has the compound word used to name **a bird that is black**?

I have **bathroom**.

Who has the compound word used to name **a plane that flies in the sky**?

I have **blackbird**.

Who has the compound word used to name **a ring worn in the ear**?

I have **airplane**.

Who has the compound word used to name **a food made out of oats**?

I have **earring**.

Who has the compound word used to say that **the earth shook**?

I have **oatmeal**.

Who has the compound word used to name **a book that holds notes**?

I Have, Who Has?: Language Arts • 1–2 © 2007 Creative Teaching Press

Compound Words 2

I have **notebook**.

Who has the compound word used to name **a coat worn over clothes**?

I have **quicksand**.

Who has the compound word used to name **corn that pops**?

I have **overcoat**.

Who has the compound word used to name **the snake with a rattle**?

I have **popcorn**.

Who has the compound word used to name **a ship that was destroyed**?

I have **rattlesnake**.

Who has the compound word used to name **a road made out of rails for a train**?

I have **shipwreck**.

Who has the compound word used to name **the light that shines in one spot**?

I have **railroad**.

Who has the compound word used to name **soft sand in which you could quickly sink**?

I have **spotlight**.

Who has the compound word used to name **a friend who is a boy**?

I Have, Who Has? Language Arts • 1–2 © 2007 Creative Teaching Press

Compound Words 2

I have **boyfriend**.

Who has the compound word used to name **a watch worn on the wrist**?

I have **suitcase**.

Who has the compound word used to name **a person on your team**?

I have **wristwatch**.

Who has the compound word used to name **the area under the ground**?

I have **teammate**.

Who has the compound word used to name **a tan from the sun**?

I have **underground**.

Who has the compound word used to name **the time the sun goes down**?

I have **suntan**.

Who has the compound word used to name **a nail on your toe**?

I have **sunset**.

Who has the compound word used to name **a case used to carry suits or clothes**?

I have **toenail**.

Who has the compound word used to name **a man who predicts the weather**?

I Have, Who Has?: Language Arts • 1–2 © 2007 Creative Teaching Press

Compound Words 2

I have **weatherman**.

Who has the compound word used to name **a game played by throwing a ball into a basket**?

I have **firewood**.

Who has the compound word used to name **a stack of hay on a farm**?

I have **basketball**.

Who has the compound word used to name **the day you were born**?

I have **haystack**.

Who has the compound word used to name **something used to scare away the crows**?

I have **birthday**.

Who has the compound word used to name **a book that tells how to cook**?

I have **scarecrow**.

Who has the compound word used to name **a game played by hitting a ball and then running bases**?

I have **cookbook**.

Who has the compound word used to name **wood used for a fire**?

I have **baseball**.

Who has the **first card**?

Name _____ Date _____

Compound Words 2

I Follow the path by coloring the compound words as your classmates name them.

*Start	airtight	firewood	haystack	*Finish
earring	blackbird	cookbook	scarecrow	baseball
earthquake	duckbill	birthday	basketball	weatherman
bathroom	airplane	oatmeal	suntan	toenail
rattlesnake	overcoat	notebook	teammate	suitcase
railroad	platypus	spotlight	boyfriend	sunset
quicksand	popcorn	shipwreck	wristwatch	underground
A	**B**	**C**	**D**	**E**

II **Fun Fact: What is the only mammal in the world that squirts venom?**

Write the words left over on the lines to answer the Fun Fact question.

Solution: ___ It's ___ ___ the ___ _____ _____

III Which word in the solution above is a compound word? _____

IV Write the words that make up two of the compound words in Column D.

1. _____ is made from _____ and _____

2. _____ is made from _____ and _____

I Have, Who Has?: Language Arts • 1–2 © 2007 Creative Teaching Press

Identify the Singular Noun

I have the **first card**.

Who has the word that means **only one of the friends**?

I have **boy**.

Who has the word that means **only one of the cars**?

I have **friend**.

Who has the word that means **only one of the balls**?

I have **car**.

Who has the word that means **only one of the things**?

I have **ball**.

Who has the word that means **only one of the cats**?

I have **thing**.

Who has the word that means **only one of the hands**?

I have **cat**.

Who has the word that means **only one of the boys**?

I have **hand**.

Who has the word that means **only one of the dogs**?

Identify the Singular Noun

I have **dog**.

Who has the word that means **only one of the flowers**?

I have **king**.

Who has the word that means **only one of the girls**?

I have **flower**.

Who has the word that means **only one of the houses**?

I have **girl**.

Who has the word that means **only one of the names**?

I have **house**.

Who has the word that means **only one of the books**?

I have **name**.

Who has the word that means **only one of the days**?

I have **book**.

Who has the word that means **only one of the kings**?

I have **day**.

Who has the word that means **only one of the ants**?

I Have, Who Has?: Language Arts • 1–2 © 2007 Creative Teaching Press

Identify the Singular Noun

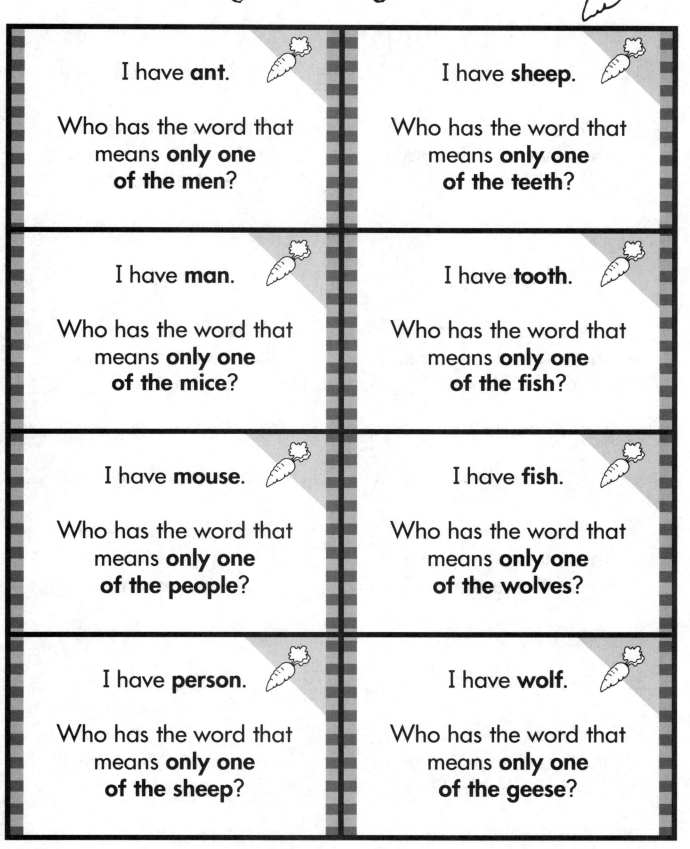

I have **ant**.

Who has the word that means **only one of the men**?

I have **sheep**.

Who has the word that means **only one of the teeth**?

I have **man**.

Who has the word that means **only one of the mice**?

I have **tooth**.

Who has the word that means **only one of the fish**?

I have **mouse**.

Who has the word that means **only one of the people**?

I have **fish**.

Who has the word that means **only one of the wolves**?

I have **person**.

Who has the word that means **only one of the sheep**?

I have **wolf**.

Who has the word that means **only one of the geese**?

Identify the Singular Noun

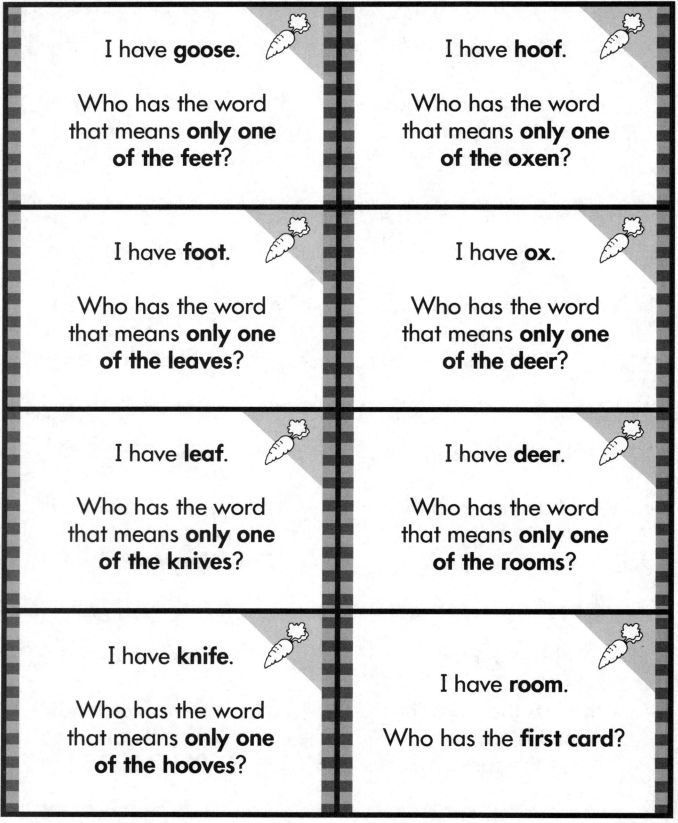

I have **goose**.

Who has the word that means **only one of the feet**?

I have **hoof**.

Who has the word that means **only one of the oxen**?

I have **foot**.

Who has the word that means **only one of the leaves**?

I have **ox**.

Who has the word that means **only one of the deer**?

I have **leaf**.

Who has the word that means **only one of the knives**?

I have **deer**.

Who has the word that means **only one of the rooms**?

I have **knife**.

Who has the word that means **only one of the hooves**?

I have **room**.

Who has the **first card**?

I Have, Who Has?: Language Arts • 1–2 © 2007 Creative Teaching Press

Name _____ Date _____

Identify the Singular Noun

I Follow the path by coloring the singular nouns as your classmates name them.

*Start	friend	ball	bat	plate
car	boy	cat	house	book
thing	hand	dog	flower	king
tooth	sheep	person	cow	girl
fish	wolf	mouse	man	name
foot	goose	table	ant	day
leaf	ox	deer	child	cookie
knife	hoof	room	*Finish	bird

II Write three of the singular nouns that are not colored in the table above. Then write the plural form of each noun.

1. _____ is the singular form of _____

2. _____ is the singular form of _____

3. _____ is the singular form of _____

I Have, Who Has? Language Arts • 1–2 © 2007 Creative Teaching Press

Identify the Plural Noun

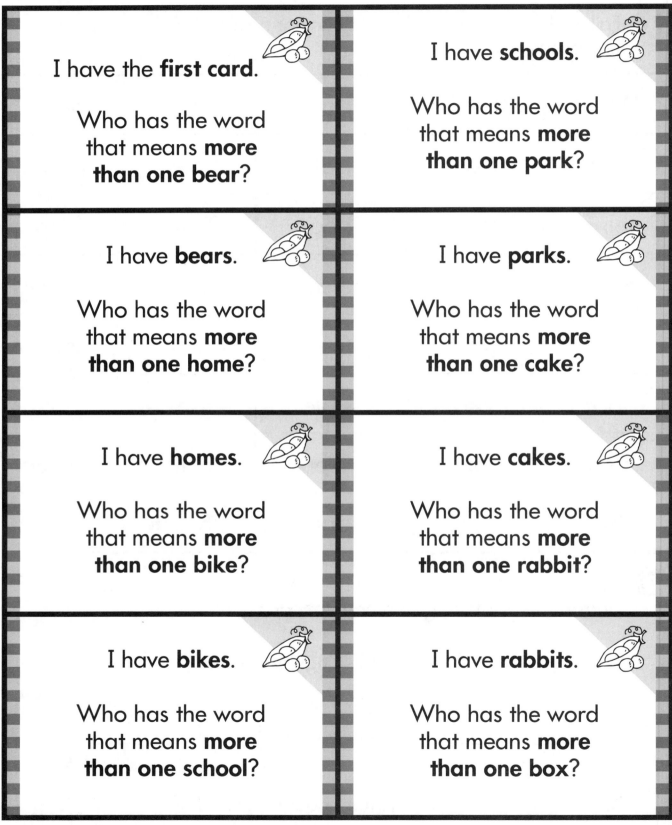

I have the **first card**.

Who has the word that means **more than one bear**?

I have **schools**.

Who has the word that means **more than one park**?

I have **bears**.

Who has the word that means **more than one home**?

I have **parks**.

Who has the word that means **more than one cake**?

I have **homes**.

Who has the word that means **more than one bike**?

I have **cakes**.

Who has the word that means **more than one rabbit**?

I have **bikes**.

Who has the word that means **more than one school**?

I have **rabbits**.

Who has the word that means **more than one box**?

I Have, Who Has?: Language Arts • 1–2 © 2007 Creative Teaching Press

Identify the Plural Noun

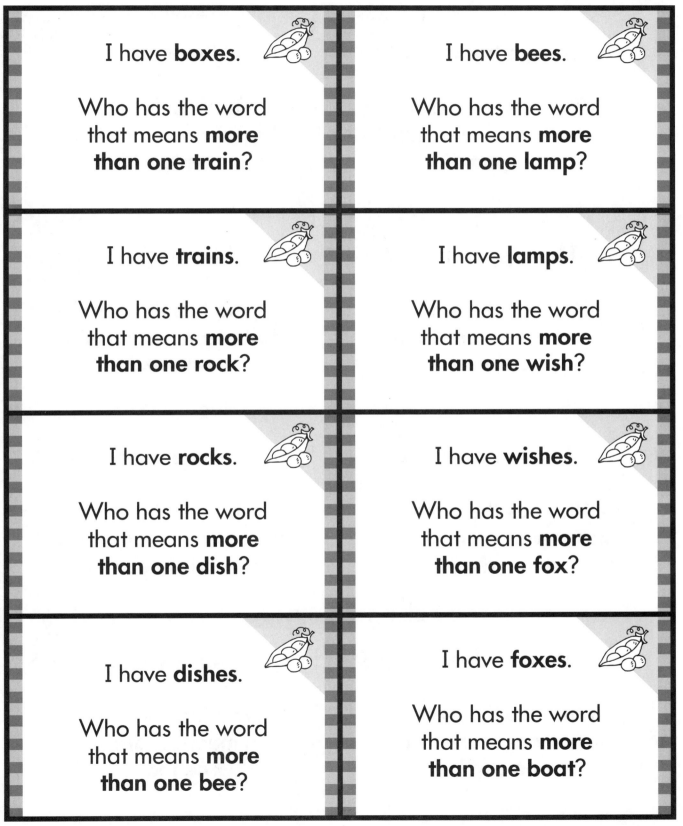

I have **boxes**.

Who has the word that means **more than one train**?

I have **bees**.

Who has the word that means **more than one lamp**?

I have **trains**.

Who has the word that means **more than one rock**?

I have **lamps**.

Who has the word that means **more than one wish**?

I have **rocks**.

Who has the word that means **more than one dish**?

I have **wishes**.

Who has the word that means **more than one fox**?

I have **dishes**.

Who has the word that means **more than one bee**?

I have **foxes**.

Who has the word that means **more than one boat**?

Identify the Plural Noun

I have **boats**.

Who has the word that means **more than one spoon**?

I have **cups**.

Who has the word that means **more than one tooth**?

I have **spoons**.

Who has the word that means **more than one clock**?

I have **teeth**.

Who has the word that means **more than one ox**?

I have **clocks**.

Who has the word that means **more than one baby**?

I have **oxen**.

Who has the word that means **more than one sheep**?

I have **babies**.

Who has the word that means **more than one cup**?

I have **sheep**.

Who has the word that means **more than one man**?

I Have, Who Has?: Language Arts • 1–2 © 2007 Creative Teaching Press

Identify the Plural Noun

I have **men**.

Who has the word that means **more than one loaf**?

I have **children**.

Who has the word that means **more than one foot**?

I have **loaves**.

Who has the word that means **more than one mouse**?

I have **feet**.

Who has the word that means **more than one fly**?

I have **mice**.

Who has the word that means **more than one goose**?

I have **flies**.

Who has the word that means **more than one cow**?

I have **geese**.

Who has the word that means **more than one child**?

I have **cows**.

Who has the **first card**?

Name _____ Date _____

Identify the Plural Noun

I Follow the path by coloring the plural nouns as your classmates name them.

*Start	cups	rocks	dishes	rats
bears	homes	trains	bees	lamps
schools	bikes	boxes	leaves	wishes
parks	cakes	rabbits	boats	foxes
mice	loaves	trees	spoons	clocks
geese	men	sheep	oxen	babies
children	feet	games	teeth	cups
ladies	flies	cows	*Finish	zoos

II Write three of the plural nouns that are not colored in the table above. Then write the singular form of each noun.

1. _____ is the plural form of _____

2. _____ is the plural form of _____

3. _____ is the plural form of _____

I Have Who Has? Language Arts • 1–2 © 2007 Creative Teaching Press

Identify the Main Idea

I have the **first card**.

Who has the main idea of these words: **red**, **purple**, **green**?

I have **weather**.

Who has the main idea of these words: **add**, **subtract**, **numbers**?

I have **colors**.

Who has the main idea of these words: **cat**, **dog**, **rabbit**?

I have **math**.

Who has the main idea of these words: **water**, **juice**, **tea**?

I have **pets**.

Who has the main idea of these words: **baseball**, **soccer**, **basketball**?

I have **things you drink**.

Who has the main idea of these words: **penny**, **nickel**, **quarter**?

I have **sports**.

Who has the main idea of these words: **rainy**, **sunny**, **cloudy**?

I have **coins**.

Who has the main idea of these words: **trout**, **cod**, **salmon**?

Identify the Main Idea

I have **fish**.

Who has the
main idea of these
words: **penguin**, **panda**,
orca whale?

I have **forms
of transportation**.

Who has the main idea
of these words: **lake**,
river, **stream**?

I have **black
and white animals**.

Who has the main idea
of these words: **cookies**,
cakes, **brownies**?

I have **bodies
of water**.

Who has the main idea
of these words: **cereal**,
eggs, **pancakes**?

I have **sweet treats**.

Who has the main idea
of these words: **cap**,
hat, **ear muff**?

I have
breakfast foods.

Who has the main idea
of these words: **shoes**,
socks, **sandals**?

I have **things you
wear on your head**.

Who has the main idea
of these words: **car**,
bike, **train**?

I have **things you
wear on your feet**.

Who has the main idea
of these words: **book**,
magazine, **newspaper**?

I Have, Who Has? Language Arts • 1–2 © 2007 Creative Teaching Press

Identify the Main Idea

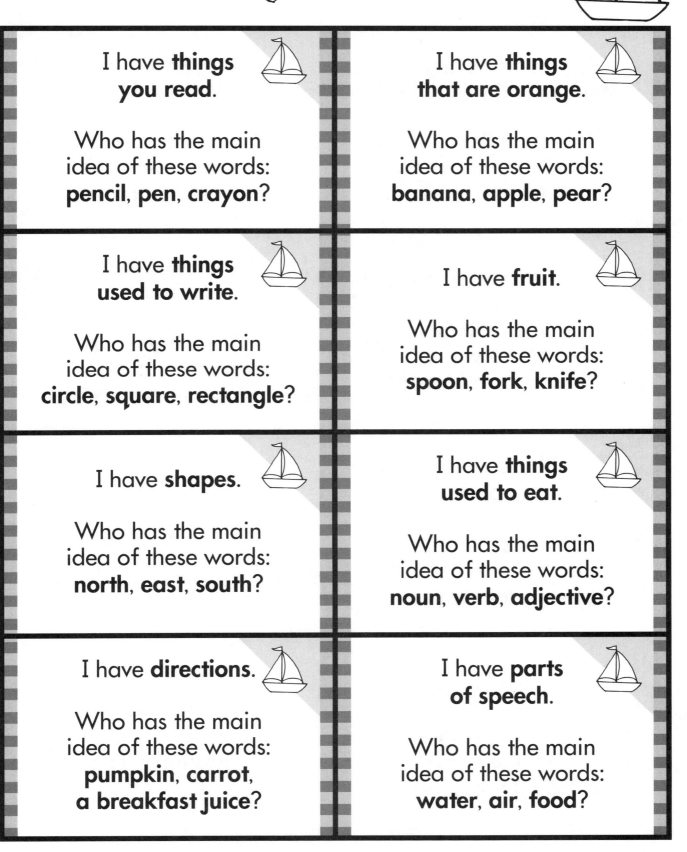

I have **things you read**.

Who has the main idea of these words: **pencil**, **pen**, **crayon**?

I have **things that are orange**.

Who has the main idea of these words: **banana**, **apple**, **pear**?

I have **things used to write**.

Who has the main idea of these words: **circle**, **square**, **rectangle**?

I have **fruit**.

Who has the main idea of these words: **spoon**, **fork**, **knife**?

I have **shapes**.

Who has the main idea of these words: **north**, **east**, **south**?

I have **things used to eat**.

Who has the main idea of these words: **noun**, **verb**, **adjective**?

I have **directions**.

Who has the main idea of these words: **pumpkin**, **carrot**, **a breakfast juice**?

I have **parts of speech**.

Who has the main idea of these words: **water**, **air**, **food**?

Identify the Main Idea

I have **what living things need to survive**.

Who has the main idea of these words: **onion**, **turnip**, **broccoli**?

I have **things you watch**.

Who has the main idea of these words: **octopus**, **shark**, **eel**?

I have **vegetables**.

Who has the main idea of these words: **two**, **six**, **and ten**?

I have **ocean animals**.

Who has the main idea of these words: **winter**, **summer**, **spring**?

I have **even numbers**.

Who has the main idea of these words: **parakeet**, **canary**, **parrot**?

I have **seasons**.

Who has the main idea of these words: **ring**, **bracelet**, **necklace**?

I have **birds**.

Who has the main idea of these words: **movie**, **play**, **television**?

I have **jewelry**.

Who has the **first card**?

Name _____ Date _____

Identify the Main Idea

I Follow the path by coloring the main ideas as your classmates name them.

*Start	colors	pets	sports	weather	math
things used to write	things you read	things you wear on your feet	sweet treats	black and white animals	things you drink
shapes	directions	breakfast foods	things you wear on your head	fish	coins
fruit	things that are orange	bodies of water	forms of transportation	ocean animals	seasons
things used to eat				things you watch	jewelry
parts of speech	what living things need to survive	vegetables	even numbers	birds	*Finish

II Write your favorite main idea from the table in the blank box above.

Identify the Details for Each Main Idea

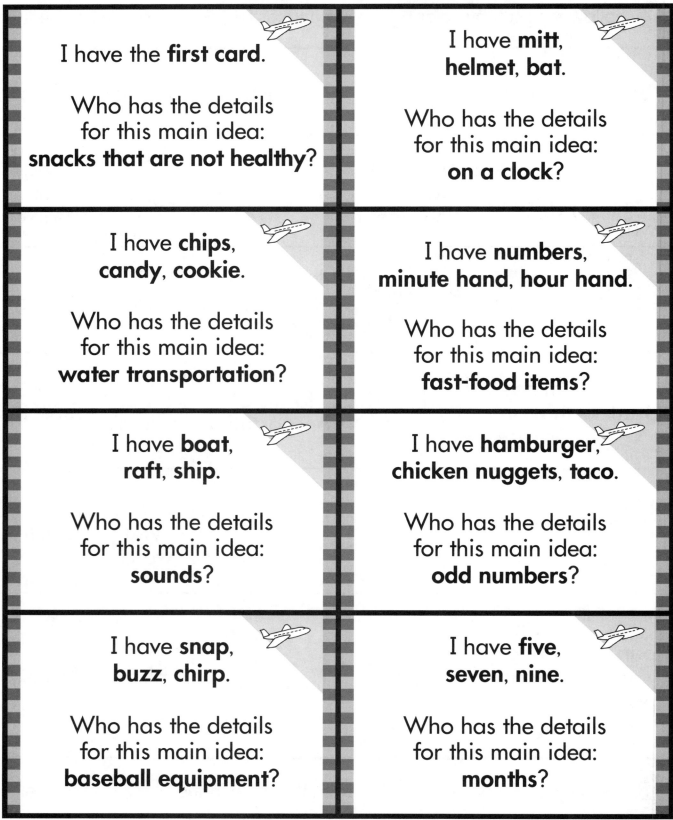

I have the **first card**.

Who has the details
for this main idea:
snacks that are not healthy?

I have **mitt**,
helmet, **bat**.

Who has the details
for this main idea:
on a clock?

I have **chips**,
candy, **cookie**.

Who has the details
for this main idea:
water transportation?

I have **numbers**,
minute hand, **hour hand**.

Who has the details
for this main idea:
fast-food items?

I have **boat**,
raft, **ship**.

Who has the details
for this main idea:
sounds?

I have **hamburger**,
chicken nuggets, **taco**.

Who has the details
for this main idea:
odd numbers?

I have **snap**,
buzz, **chirp**.

Who has the details
for this main idea:
baseball equipment?

I have **five**,
seven, **nine**.

Who has the details
for this main idea:
months?

I Have . . . Who Has? Language Arts • 1, 2, 3 © 2007 Creative Teaching Press

Identify the Details for Each Main Idea

I have **March**, June, December.

Who has the details for this main idea: **things a person does when sick?**

I have **plumber**, doctor, teacher.

Who has the details for this main idea: **types of nuts?**

I have **sneeze**, cough, sleep.

Who has the details for this main idea: **rooms in a house?**

I have **peanut**, cashew, walnut.

Who has the details for this main idea: **parts of a face?**

I have **bedroom**, kitchen, bathroom.

Who has the details for this main idea: **tools?**

I have **eyes**, nose, mouth.

Who has the details for this main idea: **heavy things?**

I have **hammer**, saw, pliers.

Who has the details for this main idea: **jobs?**

I have **bricks**, elephant, tree.

Who has the details for this main idea: **things you can fill with air?**

Identify the Details for Each Main Idea

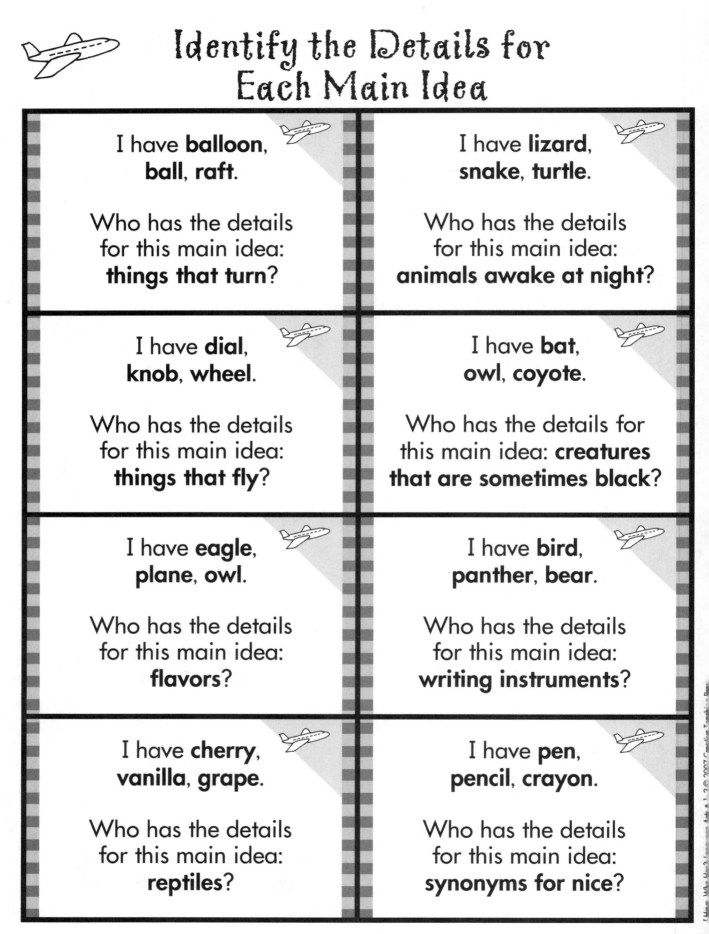

I have **balloon**, **ball**, **raft**.

Who has the details for this main idea: **things that turn?**

I have **lizard**, **snake**, **turtle**.

Who has the details for this main idea: **animals awake at night?**

I have **dial**, **knob**, **wheel**.

Who has the details for this main idea: **things that fly?**

I have **bat**, **owl**, **coyote**.

Who has the details for this main idea: **creatures that are sometimes black?**

I have **eagle**, **plane**, **owl**.

Who has the details for this main idea: **flavors?**

I have **bird**, **panther**, **bear**.

Who has the details for this main idea: **writing instruments?**

I have **cherry**, **vanilla**, **grape**.

Who has the details for this main idea: **reptiles?**

I have **pen**, **pencil**, **crayon**.

Who has the details for this main idea: **synonyms for nice?**

Identify the Details for Each Main Idea

I have **kind,
sweet, thoughtful**.

Who has the details
for this main idea:
3-D shapes?

I have **pants,
shirt, shorts**.

Who has the details
for this main idea:
computer items?

I have **cube,
pyramid, cone**.

Who has the details
for this main idea:
types of sandwiches?

I have **mouse,
keyboard, monitor**.

Who has the details
for this main idea:
creatures with sharp teeth?

I have **tuna, peanut
butter and jelly, ham**.

Who has the details
for this main idea:
items to keep bodies clean?

I have **alligator,
tiger, shark**.

Who has the details
for this main idea:
things on a calendar?

I have **soap,
shampoo, toothpaste**.

Who has the details
for this main idea:
clothing items?

I have **day, date, month**.

Who has the **first card**?

Identify the Details for Each Main Idea

I Follow the path by coloring the details as your classmates name them.

*Start	chips candy cookie	boat raft ship	soap shampoo tooth-paste	pants shirt shorts	mouse keyboard monitor	alligator tiger shark	day date month	*Finish
numbers minute hand hour hand	mitt helmet bat	snap buzz chirp	tuna peanut butter and jelly ham	cube pyramid cone	kind sweet thoughtful	pen pencil crayon	bird panther bear	It's
ham-burger chicken nuggets taco	sneeze cough sleep	bedroom kitchen bath-room	bald	eyes nose mouth	bricks elephant tree	balloon ball raft	bat owl coyote	lizard snake turtle
five seven nine	March June December	hammer saw pliers	plumber doctor teacher	peanut cashew walnut	eagle	dial knob wheel	eagle plane owl	cherry vanilla grape

II Riddle: What bird never needs a haircut?

Write the words left over on the lines below to answer the riddle.

Solution: _____ the _____ _____.

Elimination Based upon Content Categories

I have the **first card**.

Which word does not belong with the others: **happy**, **joyful**, **sad**?

I have **five**.

Which word does not belong with the others: **period**, **verb**, **adjective**?

I have **sad**.

Which word does not belong with the others: **penny**, **token**, **quarter**?

I have **period**.

Which word does not belong with the others: **flower**, **moon**, **star**?

I have **token**.

Which word does not belong with the others: **Friday**, **March**, **Tuesday**?

I have **flower**.

Which word does not belong with the others: **tiger**, **rabbit**, **cheetah**?

I have **March**.

Which word does not belong with the others: **ten**, **twenty**, **five**?

I have **rabbit**.

Which word or phrase does not belong with the others: **please, thank you, no way**?

Elimination Based upon Content Categories

I have **no way**.

Which word does not belong with the others: **winter**, **rain**, **summer**?

I have **carrot**.

Which word does not belong with the others: **beep**, **loud**, **bang**?

I have **rain**.

Which word does not belong with the others: **cup**, **gallon**, **pound**?

I have **loud**.

Which word does not belong with the others: **leg**, **mouth**, **foot**?

I have **pound**.

Which word does not belong with the others: **coffee**, **lemonade**, **hot cocoa**?

I have **mouth**.

Which word does not belong with the others: **horrible**, **terrific**, **great**?

I have **lemonade**.

Which word does not belong with the others: **carrot**, **peach**, **apple**?

I have **horrible**.

Which word does not belong with the others: **jet**, **airplane**, **train**?

Elimination Based upon Content Categories

I have **train**.

Which word does not belong with the others: **doughnut**, **wheel**, **box**?

I have **eel**.

Which word does not belong with the others: **first**, **even**, **next**?

I have **box**.

Which word does not belong with the others: **square**, **cone**, **triangle**?

I have **even**.

Which word does not belong with the others: **large**, **tiny**, **giant**?

I have **cone**.

Which word does not belong with the others: **ice cream**, **ice**, **hot cocoa**?

I have **tiny**.

Which word does not belong with the others: **salad**, **cookie**, **brownie**?

I have **hot cocoa**.

Which word does not belong with the others: **frog**, **eel**, **duck**?

I have **salad**.

Which word does not belong with the others: **tiger**, **leopard**, **kangaroo**?

Elimination Based upon Content Categories

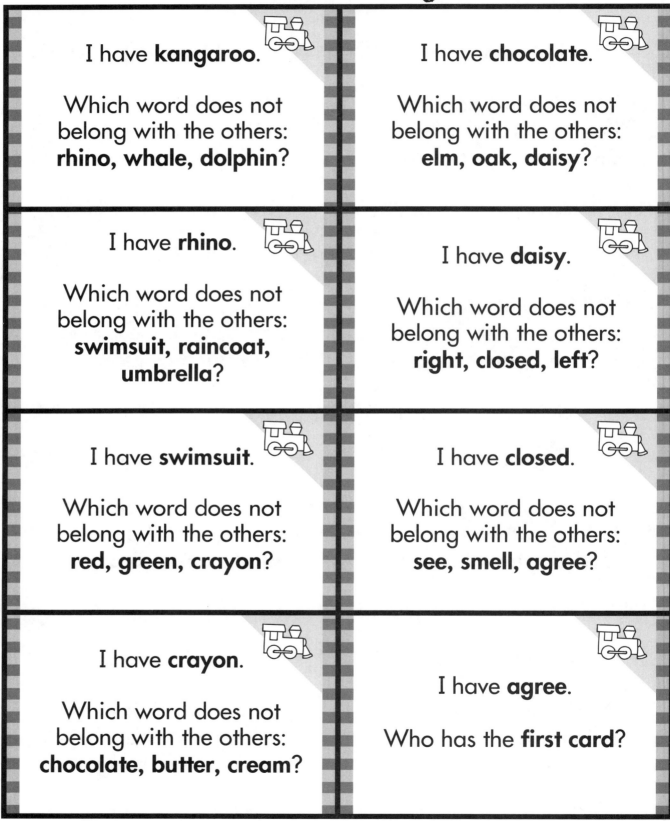

I have **kangaroo**.

Which word does not belong with the others: **rhino, whale, dolphin**?

I have **chocolate**.

Which word does not belong with the others: **elm, oak, daisy**?

I have **rhino**.

Which word does not belong with the others: **swimsuit, raincoat, umbrella**?

I have **daisy**.

Which word does not belong with the others: **right, closed, left**?

I have **swimsuit**.

Which word does not belong with the others: **red, green, crayon**?

I have **closed**.

Which word does not belong with the others: **see, smell, agree**?

I have **crayon**.

Which word does not belong with the others: **chocolate, butter, cream**?

I have **agree**.

Who has the **first card**?

Name _____ Date _____

Elimination Based upon Content Categories

I Follow the path by coloring the words as your classmates name them.

*Start	crayon	chocolate	daisy	closed	
sad	swimsuit	rhino	kangaroo	agree	
token	period	flower	salad	***Finish**	
March	five	rabbit	tiny	hot cocoa	cone
pound	rain	no way	even	eel	box
lemonade	carrot	loud	mouth	horrible	train

II Write your own set of three details in the blank box above. Include one detail that doesn't belong with the others.

III Cross out the word below that does not belong in each group. Write one sentence to explain why it does not belong in the group.

1. movies, sleep, television

   Why? _____

2. apple, banana, broccoli

   Why? _____

Elimination Based upon Phonics

(**Note:** Advise students to listen for the beginning sound that is different from the others.)

I have the **first card**.

Who has the word that does not belong with the others: **shoe**, **shine**, **chat**?

I have **chick**.

Who has the word that does not belong with the others: **wrap**, **flip**, **wrong**?

I have **chat**.

Who has the word that does not belong with the others: **when, this, that**?

I have **flip**.

Who has the word that does not belong with the others: **cling**, **chip**, **clock**?

I have **when**.

Who has the word that does not belong with the others: **chew**, **whip**, **chest**?

I have **chip**.

Who has the word that does not belong with the others: **bread**, **bring**, **crop**?

I have **whip**.

Who has the word that does not belong with the others: **chick**, **quilt**, **quit**?

I have **crop**.

Who has the word that does not belong with the others: **late**, **treat**, **lazy**?

Elimination Based upon Phonics

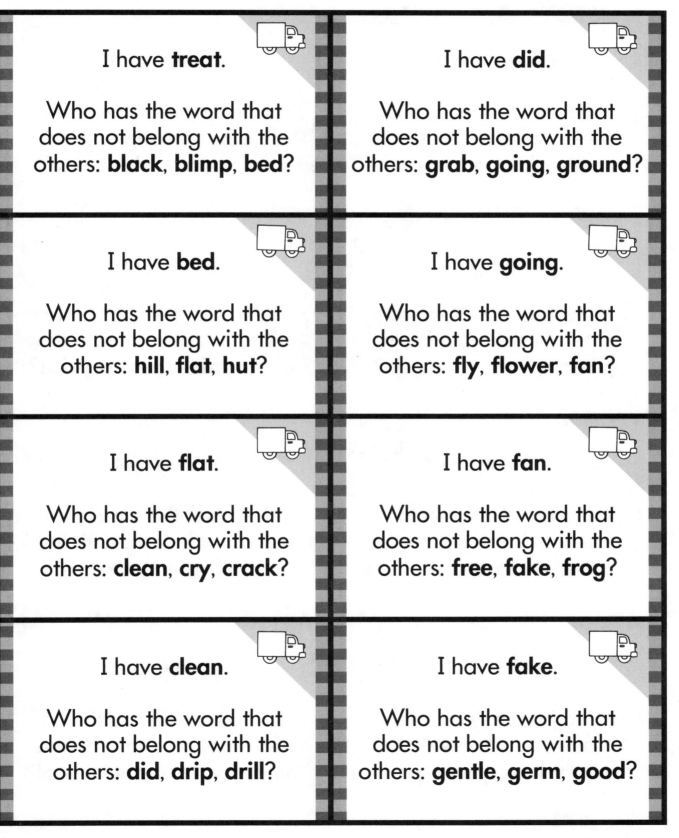

I have **treat**.

Who has the word that does not belong with the others: **black**, **blimp**, **bed**?

I have **did**.

Who has the word that does not belong with the others: **grab**, **going**, **ground**?

I have **bed**.

Who has the word that does not belong with the others: **hill**, **flat**, **hut**?

I have **going**.

Who has the word that does not belong with the others: **fly**, **flower**, **fan**?

I have **flat**.

Who has the word that does not belong with the others: **clean**, **cry**, **crack**?

I have **fan**.

Who has the word that does not belong with the others: **free**, **fake**, **frog**?

I have **clean**.

Who has the word that does not belong with the others: **did**, **drip**, **drill**?

I have **fake**.

Who has the word that does not belong with the others: **gentle**, **germ**, **good**?

Elimination Based upon Phonics

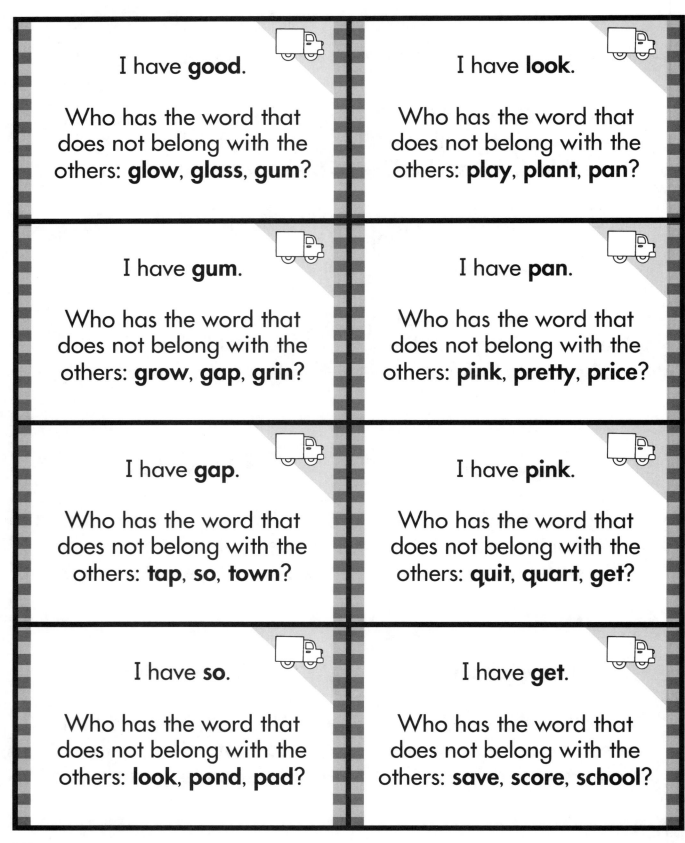

I have **good**.

Who has the word that does not belong with the others: **glow**, **glass**, **gum**?

I have **look**.

Who has the word that does not belong with the others: **play**, **plant**, **pan**?

I have **gum**.

Who has the word that does not belong with the others: **grow**, **gap**, **grin**?

I have **pan**.

Who has the word that does not belong with the others: **pink**, **pretty**, **price**?

I have **gap**.

Who has the word that does not belong with the others: **tap**, **so**, **town**?

I have **pink**.

Who has the word that does not belong with the others: **quit**, **quart**, **get**?

I have **so**.

Who has the word that does not belong with the others: **look**, **pond**, **pad**?

I have **get**.

Who has the word that does not belong with the others: **save**, **score**, **school**?

Elimination Based upon Phonics

I have **save**.

Who has the word that does not belong with the others: **sip, she, shot**?

I have **sit**.

Who has the word that does not belong with the others: **sand, spell, spot**?

I have **sip**.

Who has the word that does not belong with the others: **skin, silly, skip**?

I have **sand**.

Who has the word that does not belong with the others: **stop, sweet, star**?

I have **silly**.

Who has the word that does not belong with the others: **sing, smile, smart**?

I have **sweet**.

Who has the word that does not belong with the others: **swim, step, swing**?

I have **sing**.

Who has the word that does not belong with the others: **snug, sit, snap**?

I have **step**.

Who has the **first card**?

Elimination Based upon Phonics

I Follow the path by coloring the words as your classmates name them.

*Start	sip	silly	sing
chat	save	get	sit
when	pan	pink	sand
whip	look	so	sweet
chick	gum	gap	step
flip	good	It's	*Finish
chip	fake	fan	a
crop	hole	going	did
treat	bed	flat	clean

II **Riddle: The more you take away, the larger it gets. What is it?**

Write the words left over on the lines below to answer the riddle.

Solution: _____ _____ _____.

III Cross out the word that does not belong in each group below. Then write a sentence to explain why it does not belong.

1. silly, hungry, sad
   Why?_____

2. she, chip, chew
   Why?_____

Identify the Likely Effect

I have the **first card**.

Who has the effect for this cause: **She wanted to take a picture**?

I have **so he grabbed a tissue**.

Who has the effect for this cause: **She had to wake up early**?

I have **so she took out her camera**.

Who has the effect for this cause: **She took some medicine**?

I have **so she set her alarm clock**.

Who has the effect for this cause: **They needed to wrap some gifts**?

I have **then she felt better**.

Who has the effect for this cause: **Her hair was messy**?

I have **so they found some ribbon and gift paper**.

Who has the effect for this cause: **They wanted to save the meat for the winter**?

I have **so she brushed it**.

Who has the effect for this cause: **He was about to sneeze**?

I have **so they put it in the freezer**.

Who has the effect for this cause: **He spilled juice on his shirt**?

Identify the Likely Effect

I have **so he tried to clean it with a napkin and water**.

Who has the effect for this cause: **They could not hear him**?

I have **so he was scratching a lot**.

Who has the effect for this cause: **The lights went out in the storm**?

I have **so he started talking louder**.

Who has the effect for this cause: **There was too much fog at the airport**?

I have **so they took out the flashlights**.

Who has the effect for this cause: **The phone was ringing**?

I have **so the plane could not take off on time**.

Who has the effect for this cause: **The ape was mad**?

I have **so he picked it up and said "hello."**

Who has the effect for this cause: **The grapes were ripe**?

I have **so he started to bang on the wall**.

Who has the effect for this cause: **The dog had fleas**?

I have **so the farmers picked them**.

Who has the effect for this cause: **Her hands were dirty**?

Identify the Likely Effect

I have **so she washed them**.

Who has the effect for this cause: **The bell rang at the school**?

I have **so she ate an apple**.

Who has the effect for this cause: **They wanted to see the view like a bird**?

I have **so the children knew school was dismissed**.

Who has the effect for this cause: **A snail was in her path**?

I have **so they took a hot air balloon ride**.

Who has the effect for this cause: **He studied every night**?

I have **so she walked around it**.

Who has the effect for this cause: **The office was on the tenth floor**?

I have **so he got good grades**.

Who has the effect for this cause: **They needed stamps for the letters**?

I have **so they took the elevator**.

Who has the effect for this cause: **She wanted a piece of fruit**?

I have **so they went to the post office**.

Who has the effect for this cause: **The deer were eating her plants**?

Identify the Likely Effect

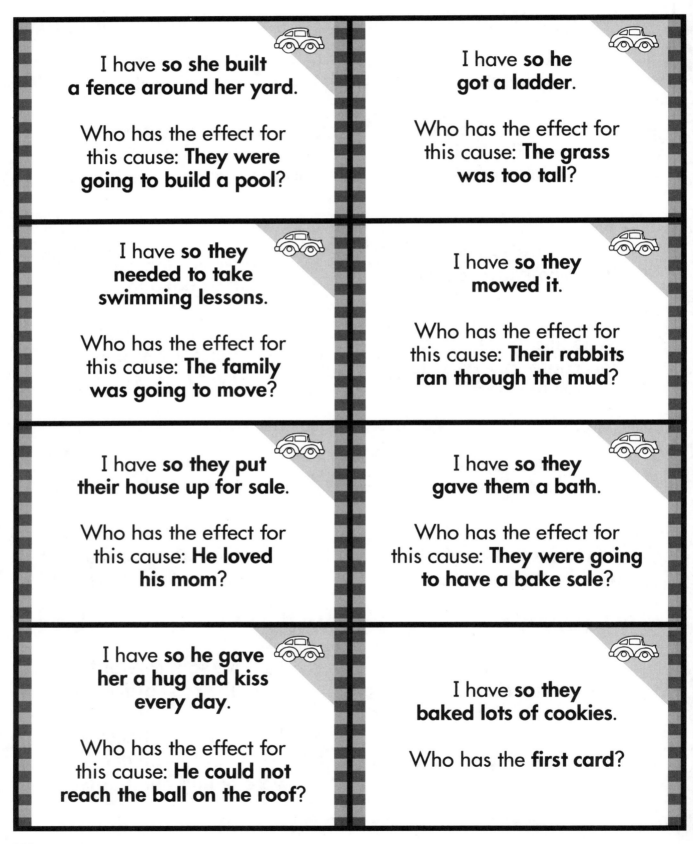

I have **so she built a fence around her yard**.

Who has the effect for this cause: **They were going to build a pool**?

I have **so he got a ladder**.

Who has the effect for this cause: **The grass was too tall**?

I have **so they needed to take swimming lessons**.

Who has the effect for this cause: **The family was going to move**?

I have **so they mowed it**.

Who has the effect for this cause: **Their rabbits ran through the mud**?

I have **so they put their house up for sale**.

Who has the effect for this cause: **He loved his mom**?

I have **so they gave them a bath**.

Who has the effect for this cause: **They were going to have a bake sale**?

I have **so he gave her a hug and kiss every day**.

Who has the effect for this cause: **He could not reach the ball on the roof**?

I have **so they baked lots of cookies**.

Who has the **first card**?

Name _____ Date _____

Identify the Likely Effect

I Follow the path by coloring the effects as your classmates name them.

*Start	She took out her camera.	She felt better.	She brushed it.	He grabbed a tissue.	She set her alarm clock.
He started to bang on the wall.	The plane could not take off on time.	He started talking louder.	He tried to clean it with a napkin and water.	They put it in the freezer.	They found some ribbon and gift paper.
He was scratching a lot.	They took out the flashlights.	He picked it up and said "hello."	The farmers picked them.	She washed them.	The children knew school was dismissed.
	*Finish	They baked lots of cookies.	She built a fence around her yard.	They went to the post office.	She walked around it.
	They mowed it.	They gave them a bath.	They needed to take swimming lessons.	He got good grades.	They took the elevator.
	He got a ladder.	He gave her a hug and kiss every day.	They put their house up for sale.	They took a hot air balloon ride.	She ate an apple.

II Circle your favorite effect from the table above. Write a different cause in the blank box.

Identify the Likely Cause

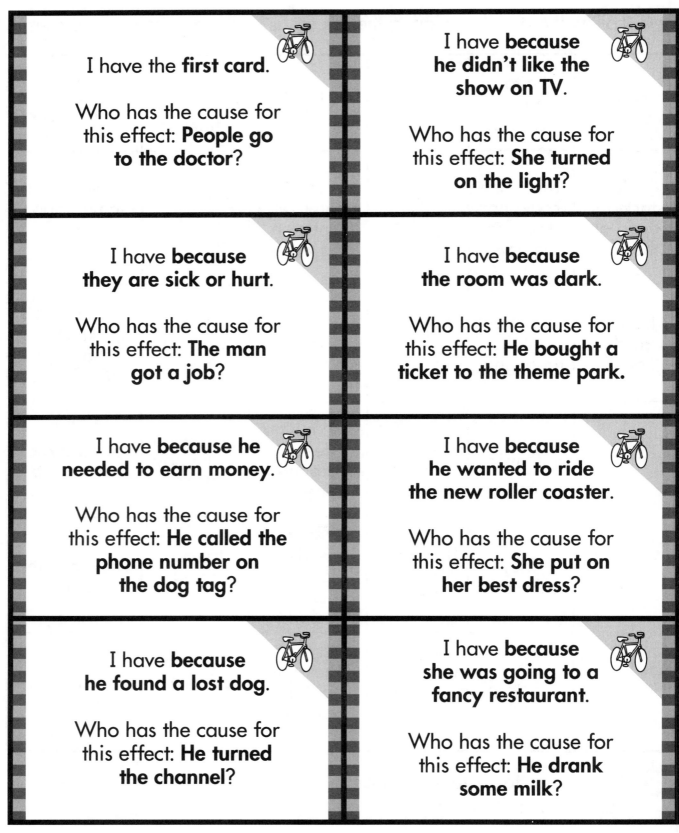

I have the **first card**.

Who has the cause for this effect: **People go to the doctor**?

I have **because he didn't like the show on TV**.

Who has the cause for this effect: **She turned on the light**?

I have **because they are sick or hurt**.

Who has the cause for this effect: **The man got a job**?

I have **because the room was dark**.

Who has the cause for this effect: **He bought a ticket to the theme park**.

I have **because he needed to earn money**.

Who has the cause for this effect: **He called the phone number on the dog tag**?

I have **because he wanted to ride the new roller coaster**.

Who has the cause for this effect: **She put on her best dress**?

I have **because he found a lost dog**.

Who has the cause for this effect: **He turned the channel**?

I have **because she was going to a fancy restaurant**.

Who has the cause for this effect: **He drank some milk**?

Identify the Likely Cause

I have **because he was thirsty**.

Who has the cause for this effect: **The baseball fans cheered**?

I have **because he wanted to build a fire in his fireplace**.

Who has the cause for this effect: **She put on her glasses**?

I have **because the player hit a home run**.

Who has the cause for this effect: **He wrote his aunt a thank-you letter**?

I have **because the words on the page looked blurry**.

Who has the cause for this effect: **She got out her joke book**?

I have **because she had sent him a gift**.

Who has the cause for this effect: **They painted the house**?

I have **because she wanted to make her friends laugh**.

Who has the cause for this effect: **He made his bed**?

I have **because the paint on the house was faded and chipped**.

Who has the cause for this effect: **He got some wood and a match**?

I have **because his bed was a mess**.

Who has the cause for this effect: **He planted a garden**?

Identify the Likely Cause

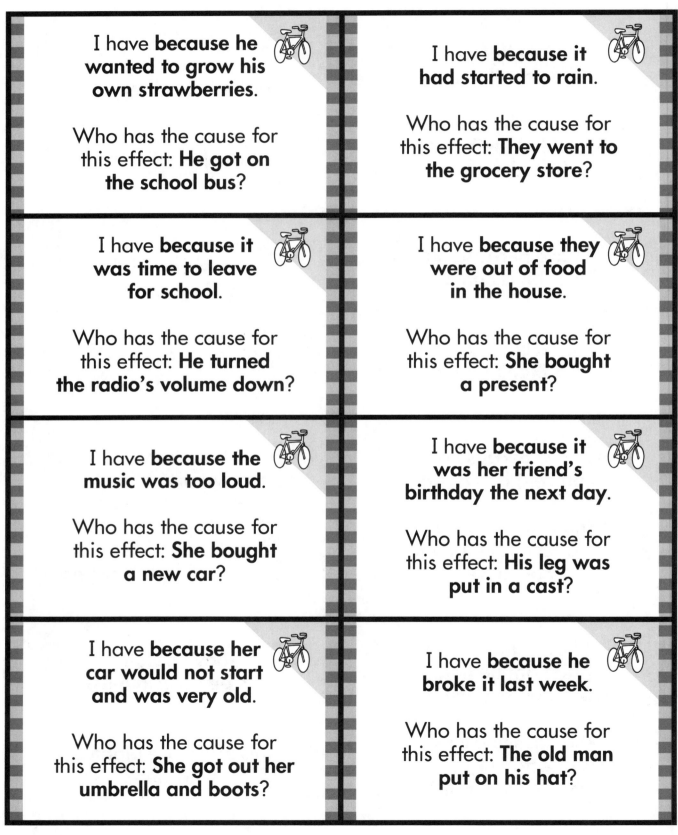

I have **because he wanted to grow his own strawberries**.

Who has the cause for this effect: **He got on the school bus**?

I have **because it had started to rain**.

Who has the cause for this effect: **They went to the grocery store**?

I have **because it was time to leave for school**.

Who has the cause for this effect: **He turned the radio's volume down**?

I have **because they were out of food in the house**.

Who has the cause for this effect: **She bought a present**?

I have **because the music was too loud**.

Who has the cause for this effect: **She bought a new car**?

I have **because it was her friend's birthday the next day**.

Who has the cause for this effect: **His leg was put in a cast**?

I have **because her car would not start and was very old**.

Who has the cause for this effect: **She got out her umbrella and boots**?

I have **because he broke it last week**.

Who has the cause for this effect: **The old man put on his hat**?

Identify the Likely Cause

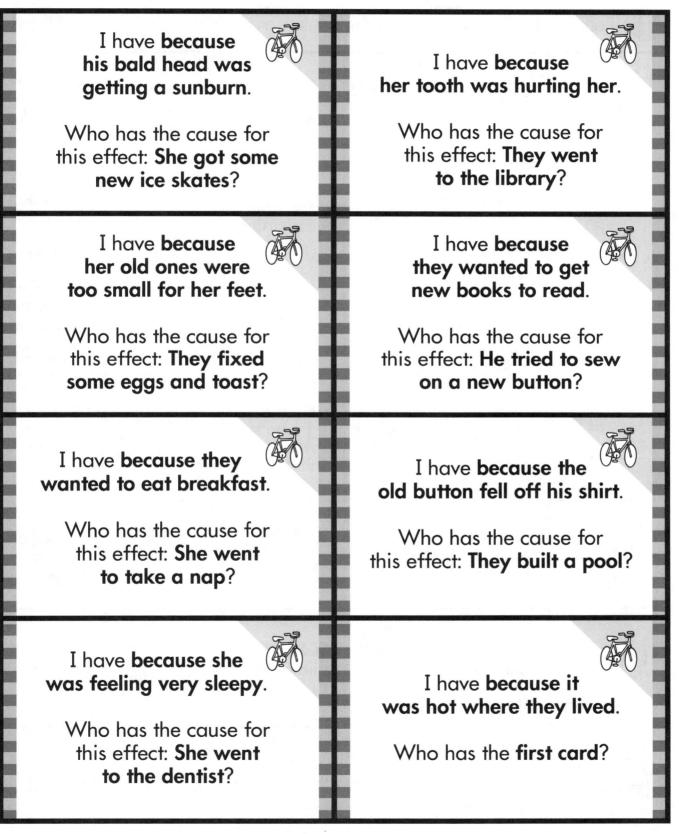

I have **because his bald head was getting a sunburn.**

Who has the cause for this effect: **She got some new ice skates?**

I have **because her tooth was hurting her.**

Who has the cause for this effect: **They went to the library?**

I have **because her old ones were too small for her feet.**

Who has the cause for this effect: **They fixed some eggs and toast?**

I have **because they wanted to get new books to read.**

Who has the cause for this effect: **He tried to sew on a new button?**

I have **because they wanted to eat breakfast.**

Who has the cause for this effect: **She went to take a nap?**

I have **because the old button fell off his shirt.**

Who has the cause for this effect: **They built a pool?**

I have **because she was feeling very sleepy.**

Who has the cause for this effect: **She went to the dentist?**

I have **because it was hot where they lived.**

Who has the **first card?**

Name _____ Date _____

Identify the Likely Cause

I Follow the path by coloring the causes as your classmates name them.

*Start	They are sick or hurt.	He needed to earn money.	He found a lost dog.	He didn't like the show on TV.	The room was dark.
	They wanted to eat breakfast.	She was feeling very sleepy.	Her tooth was hurting her.	They wanted to get new books to read.	He wanted to ride the new roller coaster.
	Her old ones were too small for her feet.	*Finish	It was hot where they lived.	The old button fell off his shirt.	She was going to a fancy restaurant.
	His bald head was getting a sunburn.	He broke it last week.	It was her friend's birthday the next day.	They were out of food in the house.	He was thirsty.
He wanted to grow his own strawberries.	It was time to leave for school.	The music was too loud.	Her car would not start and was very old.	It had started to rain.	The player hit a home run.
His bed was a mess.	She wanted to make her friends laugh.	The words on the page looked blurry.	He wanted to build a fire in his fireplace.	The paint on the house was faded and chipped.	She had sent him a gift.

II Circle your favorite cause from the table above. Write a different effect in the blank box.

Answer Key

One-Syllable Rhyming Words (Page 11)

*Start	bat	stop	free	bed
ball	trunk	fun	play	pig
fall	tail	glad	not	sack
map	snake	race	she	sing
park	smart	luck	take	hug
gave	treat	sled	sock	chin
seal	log	***Finish**	rest	ran
seed	dime	bend	hug	cat

I. Answers will vary. Possible answers include:

1. <u>ball</u> rhymes with <u>wall</u>
2. <u>snake</u> rhymes with <u>take</u>
3. <u>she</u> rhymes with <u>free</u>
4. <u>sled</u> rhymes with <u>bed</u>

Two-Syllable Rhyming Words (Page 16)

*Start	cable	measure	guppy
buckle	paddle	huddle	power
glisten	locket	flurry	mitten
cherry	lobby	travel	boulder
handle	never	money	glider
honey	double	patches	jolly
yellow	buddy	hazy	nation
collar	shiver	brother	dragon
toffee	blubber	***Finish**	manner
chowder	ranger	wiggle	flower

II. Answers will vary. Possible answers include:

1. <u>guppy</u> rhymes with <u>puppy</u>
2. <u>flurry</u> rhymes with <u>hurry</u>
3. <u>honey</u> rhymes with <u>money</u>
4. <u>hazy</u> rhymes with <u>lazy</u>

Basic Word Families (Page 21)

*Start	rug hug dug	trail snail pail	bunk trunk skunk	tap map clap	sing thing bring
say play way	pop shop hop	main pain train	feed seed weed	tin win chin	not got hot
hum drum plum				pan ran tan	fell sell well
will fill pill	sore tore chore	bed fed led	***Finish**	nest rest test	sank tank blank
luck buck stuck	few chew grew	grow slow snow	by try fly	sink drink think	sick click quick
rim brim grim	ship hip slip	rat sat flat	ham clam jam	tag rag wag	sack black rack

III. Answers will vary.

Short Vowel Word Families (Page 26)

*Start				*Finish	lip chip flip
lab tab crab	pin skin twin	lack sack black	dock flock shock	fist twist wrist	slob mob knob
hint lint sprint	hen ten when	pick trick chick	pet met wet	truck stuck duck	bend spend trend
mess dress press	pig dig twig	trash smash flash	test west chest	sad had lad	rim swim trim
clam swam tram	chant grant slant	mug tug shrug	rub tub scrub	hatch match scratch	band land stand
rod pod cod	felt pelt belt	did hid slid	fast past blast	red fed sled	spot knot got

III. Answers will vary.

Advanced Word Families (Page 36)

*Start	craft draft shaft	broth cloth sloth	paint saint quaint	roast boast toast	chimp blimp skimp
fawn lawn yawn	risk brisk whisk	math path wrath	clasp rasp grasp	bolt molt volt	talk chalk stalk
pool tool school	mask bask cask	cream stream team	camp champ stamp	dark mark shark	hedge pledge ledge
teach beach peach	fought brought thought	trait gait bait	trench wrench French	goof proof spoof	chance glance prance
coach poach broach	jaw flaw gnaw	mince wince prince			
stair fair hair	coil foil soil	cart smart start	wrong strong prong	wood hood stood	*Finish

III. Answers will vary.

Long Vowel Word Families (Page 31)

*Start	face place trace	treat heat wheat	goat float throat	flow snow grow	keep sheep sleep
kind grind blind	heal seal meal	side ride pride	mail snail quail	free bee knee	mice twice slice
grown known thrown	pipe ripe swipe	leak speak creak	rose chose those	jade shade trade	chain drain brain
need seed greed	tape grape shape	bake fake snake	reach peach bleach	hope scope slope	wife strife knife
*Finish	wage cage stage	roast boast coast	dive five drive	hike like strike	broke choke spoke
		hire tire wire	name same game	lime time slime	

III. Answers will vary.

Spelling 1 (Page 41)

→	the	and	to
in	is	he	for
you	on	at	his
of	she	by	that
with	have	from	this
they	had	do	but
not	all	were	said
when	how	use	what

II. Answers will vary.

Spelling 2 (Page 46)

→	like	many	then
some	them	make	about
look	out	more	see
into	has	him	her
way	did	get	now
call	than	down	long
day	find	these	could
would	other	take	over

II. Answers will vary.

Proper Nouns (Page 56)

*Start	The	Drake's Carpet	Shasta
Mary	Mexico	Riddle Me	Tom
Linda	MiniMart	African	Texas
May	Wednesday	Donna	B. B.'s Bakery
Weaver Elementary	Mario	Sunday	Healthy Habits
Shiloh	Ocean Ranch	Kim	October
Tuesday	Alaska	Florida	elephants
Brenton	Paul	Skate Depot	*Finish
MIND Institute	Lake Superior	Full Motorsports	Kentucky

II. Solution: The African elephants.
Proper Noun: African

Common Nouns (Page 51)

*Start	park	birds	mouse
dog	store	zoo	skateboard
rainbow	bike	tower	carnival
cake	rat	cookies	train
house	peanut butter	race	It's
movie	your	shoes	office
pool	keys	beach	homework
milkshake	car	name	book
*Finish	sunglasses	dress	bunny

II. Solution: It's your name.
Common Noun: Name

Action Verbs (Page 61)

*Start	ran	bit	blew
sold	hide	sleep	flew
read	cheered	won	chewed
dreamed	fed	drove	fixed
three	gave	left	sell
threw	heard	worked	stung
dialed	raised	asked	begged
opened	bought	kissed	towed
*Finish	baked	ride	years

II. Solution: Snails can sleep three years.
Action Verb: sleep

Verb Tenses (Page 66)

*Start	looked	dove	helped
spoke	found	kept	joined
made	ran	worked	went
chewed	sold	Stick	bought
hid	gave	fed	drove
heard	out	wanted	put
drank	watched	saw	did
held	left	tongue	called
*Finish	baked	said	took

II. Solution: Stick out your tongue.
Present Tense Verb: stick
Past Tense: stuck

Adjectives 1 (Page 71)

hot	*Start				*Finish
big	open	scary	long	curly	empty
bright	crowded	loving	calm	different	loud
round	free	hollow	dark	dirty	cheap
lazy	pretty	kind	odd	happy	friendly
green	cold	colorful	yummy	new	funny
A	B	C	D	E	F

II. Answers will vary.
III. Answers will vary.

Adjectives 2 (Page 76)

*Start	big	boiling	chubby	purring	many
damp	sticky	soft	tiny	quiet	small
straight	fluffy	enormous	noisy	antique, car	shallow
fast	young	wet	smart	first	secret
thick	respectful	popular	exciting	wise	six
filthy	helpful				*Finish

II. Answers will vary.
III. Answers will vary. Possible answers include:
1. thick
2. fluffy
3. popular
4. fast
5. noisy
6. straight

Basic Vocabulary Development (Page 81)

*Start	bike	heat	scream	plump	scent
blue	mail	well	flee	float	pal
spring	mane	cash	cart	hog	mare
stool	brake	dock	trap	crime	sty
stale	please	seed	hint	geese	throne
			*Finish	trust	flip

II. Answers will vary.
III. Answers will vary.

Advanced Vocabulary Development (Page 86)

*Start	secret	repair	mistake
every	insect	afraid	tardy
danger	locate	combine	dozen
explain	often	create	sunset
summer	tadpole	empty	wicked
creature	polite	nothing	quiet
broken	It's	hundred	subway
waiter	quickly	honest	*Finish
stranger	rotten	called	pod

II. Solution: It's called a pod.

III. Answers will vary.

Synonyms – Nouns (Page 91)

*Start	present	reward	smell	automobile	sickness
cash	soil	tale	cap	thought	infant
rug	journey	woman	youth	student	trainer
paste	floor				pair
aide	cost	evening	workout	warmth	threesome
spot	creature	bug	dawn	garbage	*Finish
A	**B**	**C**	**D**	**E**	**F**

II. Answers will vary.

III. Answers will vary. Possible answers include:
1. present is a synonym for gift
2. soil is a synonym for dirt
3. journey is a synonym for trip
4. cost is a synonym for price
5. creature is a synonym for animal

Synonyms – Verbs (Page 96)

*Start	fetch	crack	close
question	finish	cure	jump
scream	dwell	go	It's
take	desire	own	open
weep	hear	the	excuse
begin	see	soar	hold
frighten	penguin	give	laugh
thaw	blink	boast	hurry
*Finish	surprise	relax	invent

II. Solution: It's the penguin.

III. Answers will vary. Possible answers include:
1. fetch is a synonym for bring
2. finish is a synonym for complete
3. frighten is a synonym for scare

Synonyms – Adjectives (Page 101)

*Start	simple	daring	frightful	below	plump
cranky	chilly	filthy	powerful	fast	happy
delicious				right	hard
special	healthy	unhappy	*Finish	twisted	nice
slim	wealthy	new	silent	fake	tardy
thankful	tidy	little	loud	close-by	tired
A	**B**	**C**	**D**	**E**	**F**

II. Answers will vary.

III. Answers will vary. Possible answers include:
1. simple is a synonym for easy
2. chilly is a synonym for cold
3. wealthy is a synonym for rich

Synonyms – Mixed Practice (Page 106)

*Start	allow	joyful	above
It	purpose	angry	close
same	true	takes	below
smart	simple	leave	begin
aged	supper	give	aid
sleepy	skinny	task	waste
smash	clean	little	look
gather	unkind	large	create
*Finish	dozen	noisy	talk

II. Solution: It takes a dozen.

III. Answers will vary. Possible answers include:

    1. joyful is a synonym for happy

    2. simple is an synonym for basic

    3. supper is an synonym for dinner

Antonyms – Verbs (Page 116)

*Start	lose	harden	Only
go	stretch	attack	know
finish	destroy	fix	follow
listen	leave	sell	found
answer	harm	dislike	whisper
take	wake	disagree	fall
*Finish	float	close	pull
males	frown	die	thaw
gobble	stand	subtract	separate

II. Solution: Only the males gobble.

III. Answers will vary. Possible answers include:

    1. go is an antonym for stop

    2. sell is an antonym for buy

Antonyms – Nouns (Page 111)

*Start	white	student	ending	safety	boy
moonlight	fiction	sadness	answer	enemy	sunset
patient	wet	day	play	entrance	part
floor	king	child	man	cry	sister
*Finish	city	winter	follower	peace	synonym
			punishment	failure	loss
A	B	C	D	E	F

II. Answers will vary.

III. Answers will vary. Possible answers include:

    1. sunset is an antonym for sunrise

    2. sister is an antonym for brother

    3. synonym is an antonym for antonym

Antonyms – Adjectives (Page 121)

*Start	hot	soft	difficult	ugly	tall
old	west	south	bad	mean	below
full	unfair	light	polite	over	back
asleep	before	wet	smooth	outside	first
shallow	good	poor	high	huge	then
dull	odd				*Finish
A	B	C	D	E	F

II. Answers will vary.

III. Answers will vary. Possible answers include:

    1. difficult is an antonym for easy

    2. bad is an antonym for good

    3. polite is an antonym for rude

    4. smooth is an antonym for rough

Antonyms – Mixed Practice (Page 126)

*Start	outgoing	repair	dirty
together	sweet	sleep	close
out	serious	dusk	straight
costly	he	bright	praise
right	yours	eye	giving
fiction	her	fire	harsh
narrow	more	valley	light
freeze	few	far	*Finish
least	me	spend	open

II. Solution: They sleep with one eye open.

III. Antonym: wake

IV. Answers will vary. Possible answers include:

1. repair is an antonym for break
2. dirty is an antonym for clean
3. fiction is an antonym for fact

Advanced Analogies (Page 136)

*Start	foot	bookcase	book
think	green	barks	fluffy
kitchen	car	cold	see
quiet	herd	rings	hive
crawls	ostrich	sails	jungle
ocean	shoe	rough	mouth
boils	deep	bigger	wet
head	week	dirt	smells
flower	slow	*Finish	brain

II. Solution: The eye of the ostrich is bigger than its brain.

III. Answers will vary. Possible answers include:

1. envelope
2. heals
3. swims
4. slow

Basic Analogies (Page 131)

*Start	full	chair	slim	end	finish
above	white	bright	glad	heavy	night
out	shout	clear	three	south	giant
hard	subtract	hear	woman	dry	frown
question	bottom	old	learner	carry	no
pretty	sun				*Finish

II. Answers will vary.

III. Answers will vary. Possible answers include:

1. cold—antonym
2. full—antonym
3. small—synonym
4. begin—synonym

Identify the Contraction (Page 141)

A	B	C	D	E	F
*Start	I'm	he'll	where's	wasn't	I've
she'll	who's	you're	that's	isn't	haven't
didn't	let's	I'll	she's	can't	how's
it's	we've	they'll	hasn't	I'd	shouldn't
don't	what's	won't	they're	there's	he's
			*Finish	we're	you'll

II. Answers will vary.
   Possible answers include: we've, we're, we'd

III. Answers will vary. Possible answers include:
   1. I've = I + have
   2. haven't = have + not
   3. how's = how + is

Compound Words 1 (Page 151)

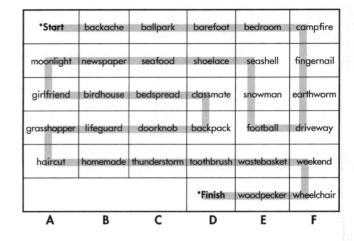

A	B	C	D	E	F
*Start	backache	ballpark	barefoot	bedroom	campfire
moonlight	newspaper	seafood	shoelace	seashell	fingernail
girlfriend	birdhouse	bedspread	classmate	snowman	earthworm
grasshopper	lifeguard	doorknob	backpack	football	driveway
haircut	homemade	thunderstorm	toothbrush	wastebasket	weekend
			*Finish	woodpecker	wheelchair

II. Answers will vary.

III. Answers will vary. Possible answers include:
   1. bedroom = bed + room
   2. seashell = sea + shell
   3. snowman = snow + man

Identify the Words for Each Contraction (Page 146)

A	B	C	D	E
*Start	I am	he is	I have	can not
who will	let us	It	we are	I will
she is	who is	we have	do not	closes
is not	has not	are not	was not	here is
she will	you are	he will	does not	they are
it is	you have	it will	its	doors
that is	you will	could not	we will	*Finish
for	two	would not	should not	months

II. Solution: It closes its doors for two months.

III. Answers will vary. Possible answers include:
   1. I + have = I've
   2. we + are = we're

Compound Words 2 (Page 156)

*Start	airtight	firewood	haystack	*Finish
earring	blackbird	cookbook	scarecrow	baseball
earthquake	duckbill	birthday	basketball	weatherman
bathroom	airplane	oatmeal	suntan	toenail
rattlesnake	overcoat	notebook	teammate	suitcase
railroad	platypus	spotlight	boyfriend	sunset
quicksand	popcorn	shipwreck	wristwatch	underground
A	B	C	D	E

II. Solution: It's the duckbill platypus.

III. Compound word: duckbill

IV. Answers will vary. Possible answers include:

  1. haystack = hay + stack
  2. scarecrow = scare + crow

Identify the Plural Noun (Page 166)

*Start	cups	rocks	dishes	rats
bears	homes	trains	bees	lamps
schools	bikes	boxes	leaves	wishes
parks	cakes	rabbits	boats	foxes
mice	loaves	trees	spoons	clocks
geese	men	sheep	oxen	babies
children	feet	games	teeth	cups
ladies	flies	cows	*Finish	zoos

II. Answers will vary. Possible answers include:

  1. cups is the plural form of cup
  2. rats is the plural form of rat
  3. leaves is the plural form of leaf

Identify the Singular Noun (Page 161)

*Start	friend	ball	bat	plate
car	boy	cat	house	book
thing	hand	dog	flower	king
tooth	sheep	person	cow	girl
fish	wolf	mouse	man	name
foot	goose	table	ant	day
leaf	ox	deer	child	cookie
knife	hoof	room	*Finish	bird

II. Answers will vary. Possible answers include:

  1. bat is the singular form of bats
  2. plate is singular form of plates
  3. cow is the singular form of cows

Identify the Main Idea (Page 171)

*Start	colors	pets	sports	weather	math
things used to write	things you read	things you wear on your feet	sweet treats	black and white animals	things you drink
shapes	directions	breakfast foods	things you wear on your head	fish	coins
fruit	things that are orange	bodies of water	forms of transportation	ocean animals	seasons
things used to eat				things you watch	jewelry
parts of speech	what living things need to survive	vegetables	even numbers	birds	*Finish

II. Answers will vary.

Identify the Details for Each Main Idea (Page 176)

*Start	chips candy cookie	boat raft ship	soap shampoo toothpaste	pants shirt shorts	mouse keyboard monitor	alligator tiger shark	day date month	*Finish
numbers minute hand hour hand	mitt helmet bat	snap buzz chirp	tuna peanut butter and jelly ham	cube pyramid cone	kind sweet thoughtful	pen pencil crayon	bird panther bear	It's
hamburger chicken nuggets taco	sneeze cough sleep	bedroom kitchen bathroom	bald	eyes nose mouth	bricks elephant tree	balloon ball raft	bat owl coyote	lizard snake turtle
five seven nine	March June December	hammer saw pliers	plumber doctor teacher	peanut cashew walnut	eagle	dial knob wheel	eagle plane owl	cherry vanilla grape

II. Solution: It's the bald eagle.

Elimination Based upon Content Categories (Page 181)

*Start	crayon	chocolate	daisy	closed	
sad	swimsuit	rhino	kangaroo	agree	
token	period	flower	salad	*Finish	
March	five	rabbit	tiny	hot cocoa	cone
pound	rain	no way	even	eel	box
lemonade	carrot	loud	mouth	horrible	train

II. Answers will vary.

III. Answers will vary. Possible answers include:

  1. sleep—Sleep is not something you watch.
  2. broccoli—Broccoli is not a fruit.

I Have, Who Has? Language Arts • Level 2 • © 2007 Creative Teaching Press

Elimination Based upon Phonics (Page 186)

*Start	sip	silly	sing
chat	save	get	sit
when	pan	pink	sand
whip	look	so	sweet
chick	gum	gap	step
flip	good	It's	*Finish
chip	fake	fan	a
crop	hole	going	did
treat	bed	flat	clean

II. Solution: It's a hole.

III. Answers will vary. Possible answers include:

1. Hungry; The other words begin with the letter s.
2. She; The other words begin with ch.

Identify the Likely Cause (Page 196)

*Start	They are sick or hurt.	He needed to earn money.	He found a lost dog.	He didn't like the show on TV.	It was dark.
	They wanted to eat breakfast.	She was feeling very sleepy.	Her tooth was hurting her.	They wanted to get new books to read.	He wanted to ride the new roller coaster.
	Her old ones were too small for her feet.	*Finish	It was hot where they lived.	The old button fell off his shirt.	She was going to a fancy restaurant.
	His bald head was getting a sunburn.	He broke it last week.	It was her friend's birthday the next day.	They were out of food in the house.	He was thirsty.
He wanted to grow his own strawberries.	It was time to leave for school.	The music was too loud.	His car would not start and was very old.	It had started to rain.	The player hit a home run.
His bed was a mess.	She wanted to make her friends laugh.	The words on the page looked blurry.	He wanted to build a fire in his log cabin.	The paint on the house was faded and chipped.	She had sent him a gift.

II. Answers will vary.

Identify the Likely Effect (Page 191)

*Start	She took out her camera.	She felt better.	She brushed it.	He grabbed a tissue.	She set her alarm clock.
He started to bang on the wall.	The plane could not take off on time.	He started talking louder.	He tried to clean it with a napkin and water.	They put it in the freezer.	They found some ribbon and gift paper.
He was scratching a lot	They took out the flashlights.	He picked it up and said "hello."	The farmers picked them.	She washed them.	The children knew school was dismissed.
	*Finish	They baked lots of cookies.	She built a fence around her yard.	They went to the post office.	She walked around it.
	They mowed it.	They gave them a bath.	They needed to take swimming lessons.	He got good grades.	They took the elevator.
	He got a ladder.	He gave her a hug and kiss every day.	They put their house up for sale.	They took a hot air balloon ride.	She ate an apple.

II. Answers will vary.